THE REAL ENEMY
(The Inner-Me)

Special Thanks and Acknowledgements

Thanks to God, the Creator of my life, for creating the life of my mother whose love and determination taught me never to give up; my children who are the fuel of my determination and who hold a special place in my heart and soul; my wife, family and friends who encourage me along this journey; and to my passed beloved grandfather Lawrence McKinley, Jr. who helped save my life and whose spirit of order, understanding, wisdom, and charity now lies within me to pass on to my children and others. Thanks for believing in me.

Editor's Note

As a child growing up in upstate New York, my parents took me to see my grandparents every weekend. I remember sitting around the kitchen table and listening to my grandfather tell stories. The stories made us mostly laugh, but also get upset, express empathy, and allowed us to bond with each other. His personal experiences shaped who we were as people and guided the decisions we made throughout life. That, along with other experiences I've had since then, help me realize how the wisdom others can share should not be pushed away, but instead welcomed. A person can learn a great deal from others who have been through it and even though we're not all the same, we can pick and choose bits of wisdom that will help us lead fuller lives. Knowing that we're not all that different from each other can also help us forgive, even ourselves.

Anthony's choice to use his personal experiences to better the lives of others is admirable. His history provides him with wisdom worthy of sharing and is needed for young adults to make positive choices. Anyone who picks up this book can use his stories as a reflection for themselves and hopefully will make positive changes in order to grow.

Erikka Miller lives in Tucson, Arizona with her son and boyfriend. When she is not working or being a mom, she enjoys various crafts and reading Margaret Atwood novels.

All Rights Reserved
Library of Congress Catalog Card Number TXu 1-928-423
This Certificate issued under the seal of the Copyright Office in accordance with title 17, United States Code, attest that registration has been made for the title work "The Real Enemy (My Inner- Self)". The information on this certificate has been made a part of the Copyright Office records.
No part of this publication may be reproduced or transmitted in any form or by any means, mechanical or electronic, including photocopying for recording, or by any information storage and retrieval system, without express written permission from the publisher.
ISBN: 978-0-578-15611-8
ISBN: 978-1-4951-3840-9 (ebook)

Copyright © 2012 by Anthony D. McKinley

Cover Design by Daniel Slater

Author's Remarks

My name is Anthony D. McKinley and I am a person who desires to be loved and to love others. The search was not easy, but I ultimately found love. It was only after I discovered the essence of myself and was able to answer the questions, "Who am I?" and "Where did I come from?" and identify areas I needed to improve to reach my destiny. After answering these questions the search begin to discovery myself.

As a child, my brother and I were placed in foster care and under guardianship due to the fact that someone put a "mickey," or date-rape drug, in our mother's drink, which caused her to become a "paranoid schizophrenic" and she was not able to take care of us as a parent would love to do. Although we were in the custody of others, my mother never forgot us and I can remember the many attempts she made to visit us. Our experience was not a pleasant foster care experience but I made it out, without a plan, and I knew I had to be FREE of the physical and mental pain that I endured. Looking back, I realized that it was these experiences that answer why I am the way I am. It was not easy but I needed to learn how to love those that misused me and to turn my enemies into my footstools. This is called "survival of the fittest," a statement coined by Herbert Spencer, which means that survival training is needed for all human beings, but not necessary in the manner of my experience. Survive is what we are born to do from birth. If you are reading this book, then you survived your first training, which was being birthed from your mother's womb. There is a thin line between life and death for both the mother and the child or children during the pregnancy time to the delivery. When we are born we are built to pass any test, but you have to know that with confidence. Life is filled with endless training, so be readily prepared to learn and don't make the same mistakes twice.

My personal life is a composite of experiences like everyone else. I am YOU. Although we are different and have never met, we all have the same profound need for life, which is to be LOVED. This search is never ending until we discover it for ourselves and in the book it is my intention to assist with the discovery of you and to seeing life differently.

As a teen and young man, I blamed others for my lack of having and knowing. I was envious and jealous and disliked people, period, because of how I was treated and I can say I didn't know better. Living a life in foster care under those negative mental and behavioral conditions misled me and caused me to have a false perception about life, people, and myself. I came to the realization that I mistreated all people with dislike and distrust just because of my hurt. Looking back and reflecting, I realized that I caused a lot of bad things for myself. Today, I live by two principles: what you sow is what you will reap and treat people the way you want to be treated. These are statements I feel are very important to understand in order to appropriately treat others as individuals. It also suggests you stop blaming others for your actions.

Today as an adult, I know both my mother and father, I have siblings, I am married, I have children, and I see things differently because all my life experiences including college and career opportunities. Things that conditioned me were my passion for change, my personal beliefs, my dreams and desires, my family, mentors, and educational training.

My Motto Principal Statements:

The following statements are my personal writing that I needed to help me on my journey and it helped me develop the core purpose of my writing.
Each statement suggests a state of mind and behavior to realize my POWER. This POWER is within all of us and it aids in everything from personal healing to changing the perception about self, life, and others. We all have the POWER to change and better ourselves.
Discover your POWER within!

Statement	Behavior
Desire to Love	The desire for love is so imperative that if it is not filled correctly with genuine love, then any substitute that appears and feels like love will be acceptable.
Destiny	I am on my way. I may not know my final destination; however, I have had a preview and now I know I'm bound for greatness because I AM SOMEBODY.
Self – Control	If it is to be then it is up to me to make a difference in my own life and then share it with others
Better Vision	Change your perception, change your behavior, and change your understanding about life. Nothing is impossible!
YET	YET pre-propose things to come but you have to produce something for it to come.
Selfish	When it comes to your wellbeing, career, and lifestyle it is a selfish act. Your life is a selfish act and no one will give it to you.
Conditions	Your condition of life today doesn't mean it will be your future, but is part of you as you strive for your destiny

Table of Contents:

Summary: The Real Enemy 6

Chapter 1: The Essences of Life *We are born from*............................... 9
    Where did I come from?.. 11
    Who am I?.. 13

Chapter 2: Understanding *Obedience and Honor*............................... 18
    No Plan, No Progress, No Future.. 21
    Believing In Yourself.. 24

Chapter 3: Abide *Follow the Rules*... 30
    Parental Law.. 31
    The Law... 32

Chapter 4: Discovery *Know Thyself*... 36

Chapter 5: Your Roots *Remember to Come Back to the Middle* 44

Chapter 6: The Battle *The Enemy is my Inner-Self*............................... 47
    The Enemy "The Battle Within".. 49
    Transferable Behavior: Adolescent Years....................................... 49

Chapter7: Mental Entrapment... 52
    Selfish Acts... 55

Chapter8: Releasing Mental Entrapment... 62

Chapter 9: Moments *My Gift to the Reader* 67

***Bonus*: Encouraging and Motivational Words by Anthony McKinley**................... 69

Summary

The Real Enemy
The Inner-Me

Summary

The Real Enemy
The Inner-Me

The Real Enemy is a self-help book that is designed to raise the awareness of how we get in the way of ourselves and lose sight of the greater power within. Our Real Enemy is our INNER-ME.

The Real Enemy's purpose is to analyze the transition from childhood to adulthood and realize how in some ways we sabotage and cause affliction to ourselves. This may be because of different experiences through conditional learning and personal situations that occurred which influence and affect our lives as innocent victims.

The book acts as a counseling session; the reader should gain something new and helpful. The book is designed to assist with obtaining a new perception.
I attempt to give suggestions that may help with identifying hurtful or misleading experiences and introduce readers to a positive outlook and how to possibly prevent negativity from occurring.

The challenge for most people is admitting that something is wrong or it could be one's own fault, and what I want the reader to understand is that no one should have to live their life in the shadow of hurt, lies, and secrets.

Identifying the cause and possible solutions is essential to preventing negativity from occurring throughout a person's entire life. Now is the time for you to let go of the conditions that are hurting both mentally and physically.

Coming from a harsh and unruly background that was filled with lies, contradiction, and manipulation as well as abuse both mentally and physically, I had to discover my worth and I adopted these statements for myself to live by. I have shared these with many youth and adults that I have mentor or counseled: "The condition of life doesn't mean it is the result of my destiny" and "I may not know my destiny in full scope, but I know that my current conditions are the stepping stones to my destiny."

It is imperative to identify some situations that occur and I hope to give suggestions for how to overcome those obstacles. It is my opinion that as children, adolescents, or young adults, their parents and grandparents, foster parents, guardians, and community leaders/speakers will assist with working through the

The Real Enemy - *The Inner-Me*

communication process and prevent negative situations from occurring.
The book originates from my personal notes and behavior, life lessons learned, my educational experience, my nonprofit organization named, Youth Outreach Summit, Inc., and my foster care experiences that I was able to overcome because of exposure, and a desire to live life free from my Real Enemy which is me.

The overall purpose for reading this book is to reflect, learn, and prevent some things from occurring again. Also, it's important to realize that we all make mistakes, but to keep doing it over and over again is a form of insanity. Please move out of your own way, let the past be the past, and have confidence that you can change your current situation if you change how you see it. Admit to your wrongdoing and decide to CHANGE in order to win your life back with a new perception. You are worth the work you invest into YOU.

Peace, Love and Willpower.

Chapter 1

The Essences of Life
We are born from...

Chapter 1

The Essences of Life
We are born from…

Question!
One of the most asked questions in life is, "Is there is a God?" In my opinion, each person has to discover the answer for him or herself.

Food for thought!
It is evident that we as human beings have the ability to procreate and the ability to manufacture and invent new things for the advancement of humanity.
If human beings can do these things from our thoughts and behaviors, then someone with all-superior creative powers must be present. There is nothing that comes from itself! That statement implies that someone or something created everything as it pertains to the world and human beings.

Suggestive Theory:
Life began in the mind of a spiritual supreme being known as the Creator, or God. The Creator designed and established everything with hope, grace, freewill and love. I believe the Creator created human beings to be unique for companionship and to love one another with our differences. Simply, companionship is established only for communication and achievement. Communication is the expression and exchange of thoughts to empower and be a catalyst for positive behavior. Achievement is established to encourage each person to strive to accomplish a variety of things for internal change and maturation. The power of both communication and achievement manifest in love and love overrules all evil intentions and negative forces. Creating positive behavior, thoughts, and speaking positively is very important to how you view things, feel about self, and other people. You can influence more people with positive energy and behavior, even when things are not going your way.

I believe the Creator placed the ability to communicate, achieve, and love innately within each of us in order to persevere to accomplish our individual destinies.
As individuals we need to realize that we all born with unique abilities.
However, we are each given the choice to discover and use our abilities for the greater good toward all mankind. Our failures are shortcomings designed to teach us how to reinvent behaviors for more positive outcomes.

Note: *This is my understanding of the essences of life. Respect to all!*

The Real Enemy - *The Inner-Me*

Exercise: 👉

Please take the time to identify and reflect on your gifts, talents and skills. Those gifts, talents and skills are unique abilities that the Creator gave to you. Write them down on the lines below and write beside them how you can use them for yourself or others.

_____
_____
_____
_____
_____
_____
_____
_____
_____
_____
_____
_____
_____
_____
_____
_____
_____
_____

Successful Thoughts:

The power of the mind is as small or as large as we know and conceptualize.

Being able to make decisions about your life is essential and imperative to self and you should be careful about who you allow in your personal circle.

*To see more encouraging and motivational thoughts go to page **69**.*

The Real Enemy - *The Inner-Me*

━ Where did I come from? ━
Start at the beginning and you will find the ending the same.

There are many contradicting theories that explain the creation of man, but I will share with you mine in layman's terms. I believe that we are all created from a spiritual superior being known as the Creator or God. I believe that there is a superior being that created and allowed the first human being to exist. Everyone must search for the truth and discover the answer for self. I believe the Creator crafted us with a dual nature: spiritual and physical.

The spiritual nature is the inner force that causes us to have a heightened sense of thinking and achieving. For example, when we feel like giving up there is a drive within us that allows for heightened focus which results in our doing something that is unbelievable to many. Others may respond with, "Wow! How did he do that?"

The physical component to humanity is through a mother's womb, which creates the physical human being.

We are all created in a unique image with varying physical attributes. I believe we all have similarities and we are all connected through our life's experiences and mystic spiritual connection. For instance, all human beings come from their mother's womb, which is known as the belly of life. While we were inside, life began, and the physical and mental development began its processes. This process is the beginning of the development a human being. This is where the physical attributes, both internal and external, take to form a child.

Nine months later, a child is born into the world. The creation of every child is good, but the reality is, we live in a world comprised of both positive and negative elements that affect each person's life. Contradicting elements that are encountered in one's life are good and bad, right and wrong, happy and sad, prosperity and poverty, and love and hate. As individuals, we are conditioned by what we are taught and exposed to as we grow and develop, and each of our behaviors is a response to that condition.

Although we learn from conditions both positive and negative, we have the power to change. My grandfather would say to me, "The only things that can overcome any condition are time, the will, and something new to do in its place." He would end by saying, "Nothing is impossible if you put your mind to it." The conditions of the world are only conditions, but they don't have to determine your outcome. These conditions change because of love. Love is the ability to take care of yourself in a positive manner and to treat others the same way: out of love. Love is unconditional which means there are no circumstances that will stop you from loving yourself and others.

The Real Enemy - *The Inner-Me*

Some attributes of love include: Love does not cause hurt or pain to yourself or others. Love will allow you to tell the truth to others and find a way to be respectful.

There is one word that surpasses all others and that is love. Love is selfish when it comes to personal achievements. Love is constructive when others are giving advice to help you. Love is benevolence, not vanity. Love is affectionate and not harsh. Love is patience and kindness. Love is letting go of others, habits, and things when they appear to be pleasant but in fact are harmful and self-destructive. Love does not cost anything. Love is understood as charity. Love is the only word that gives: it exudes peace and a greater understanding.

We are all created out of love! Love is the beauty that resides in every human being.

Notes:
Regardless of your current situation, we were all born into this world for a purpose and to love and enjoy life with a peace of mind and a sense of self-accomplishment.

Do some people need more love than others? Yes! Because everyone comes from different backgrounds and family structures, there is a greater need for some to have more positive people surrounding them. Why? The more positive influences they have, the greater the chances of them making it are.

Lastly, remember life is not perfect but it is fair and you have to surround yourself around people of like minds to do something positive. What you establish for yourself before your death is entirely up to you. How you cultivate your surroundings is a reflection of your image and reputation (or representation) of who you are as a human being.

Exercise: 👉

Think about those who you are around such as friends, family members and coworkers. How do they influence your life in a positive way?
How will their influence help you meet your goals in life?

Individual Names	Relationship	How do they influence your life in a positive way?	What goal will they help you to accomplish?

The Real Enemy - *The Inner-Me*

> **Successful Thoughts:**
>
> Being selfish about your goals, ambition, and inspirations about your life is not something to be ambiguous about, but it should be something that is of importance and accomplishment for self.
>
> Love is the ability to take care of yourself in a positive manner and to treat others the same way: out of love.
>
> *To see more encouraging and motivational thoughts go to page **69**.*

◆ Who am I? ◆
I AM….

"Who am I?" is a frequently asked question throughout the world and since the beginning of time. Discovering who you are, is something that all of us must discover for ourselves to empower self, family, others, and community.
One evident way of knowing who someone is, is by observing how they respond to the question. Most of the time it is seen through the behaviors that have manifested as a result of their choices. How is it that others can tell you who you are, but you can't see that character or even that person? Primarily, we are doers and not watchers of oneself, which is perfectly fine. Doing things you enjoy in life is the passion that drives us all to do well in life regardless of our personal situations and circumstances.

Exercise: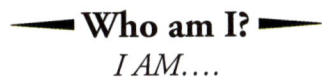

Name some activities you like doing that make you happy.
Why do they make you happy? Are you able to do these things daily, weekly, monthly or annually?

What makes you happy?	Why does it make you happy?	How often do you participate in those activities?

The Real Enemy - *The Inner-Me*

> **Successful Thoughts:**
>
> If it is to be it is up to me to make life better.
>
> Search within yourself and discover your desires and dream and make them your reality.
>
> *To see more encouraging and motivational thoughts go to page **69**.*

The question, "Who am I?" is similar to, "Where did I come from?" but is different in context and character. It is asking you, the person, what is your role in life and what are you going to do about it. Again, no one really knows the answer until we are dead and then again only the living left behind will know that. One thing that is certain is that all human beings have character. The philosopher Heraklitos once stated, "A person's character is their fate." Our character is a reflection of who we really are as human beings, and as human beings we must continue to strive to both continually and daily to become a role model for self and others.

Who am I? We are contributors to life; we are doers and not hearers only; we are leaders who create paths for others; we are makers and inventors for new discoveries; we are one of many; we are new that one day will be the old; we are the good that must overcome evil; we are boys and girls who will one day be considered men and women.

Exercise: 👉

Reflect over your life…What have you done to make someone else happy? How do you know you made them happy? If you could, would you do it again and why?

What have you done to make someone else happy?	How do you know you made them happy?	Would you do it again if you had an opportunity?
Why would you do it again?	What positive impact did those things have on you?	

The Real Enemy - *The Inner-Me*

> **Successful Thoughts:**
>
> Please move out of you on way, let the past be the past and that you can change your current situation if you change how your see it, admit to your wrong doing and deciding to CHANGE and win your life back with a New Perception. You are worth the work you invest into YOU.
>
> *To see more encouraging and motivational thoughts go to page **69**.*

Who am I? We are all human beings striving to become upright and law-abiding citizens, to prove to self, parents, family, authority figures and to the Creator that we can overcome anything that we are challenged by. As human beings we must face all of life's endeavors with the understanding that our challenges are our fears that must be conquered as each encounter occurs throughout life. One of the ways to conquer our fears and stay balanced with life is to set goals for ourselves and understand that the goals we set are the goals we achieve out of passion, joy, love, and peace.

Exercise: 👉

Write down some personal goal that you have for yourself. Have you thought about how long it will take you to accomplish your goals? Have you considered what steps to take to reach those goals? Why did you choose these as your personal goals? What is the expected positive result in fulfilling the goals that you have identified? This is a good time to write some ideas and steps to help you move forward in reaching and accomplishing your personal goals.

Personal Goals	How long will it take to accomplish this goal?	What are some steps that you need to accomplish the goal?

Why did you choose this as a personal goal?	What is your expected positive result once you meet your goal?	

The Real Enemy - *The Inner-Me*

Note: *You are your achievements with great responsibilities and success and you are the mistakes you make along the way. As human beings we must learn to accept the good with the bad things that we do, with the understanding that each of us must learn from our mistakes and never fall for the same mistake twice. We must expand on the successes so there is no room for being comfortable. Being comfortable is like waiting on someone. You don't need to stop what you're doing to reach your goals, instead continuously work to achieve them.*

As humans we need to understand more than anything that everyone is placed here on Earth in community, showing real love toward one another through respect, understanding, charity, and love.

Successful Thoughts:

Peace, Love and Will Power is a secret formula for success.

The conditions of the world are only conditions, but they don't have to determine your outcome. These conditions change because of love.

Love is the ability to take care of yourself in a positive manner and to treat others the same way: out of love.

*To see more encouraging and motivational thoughts go to page **69**.*

Chapter 2

Understanding:
Obedience and Honor

Chapter 2

Understanding:
Obedience and Honor

Obedience is the act of obeying someone's authority (e.g., parents, family, teachers, and supervisors). To be obedient requires discipline, and discipline requires self-control.

As youngsters, we would like to believe that our experiences are so different from our parents, guardians, grandparents and teachers. We believe in the statement, "Parents just don't understand," by Will Smith, but the reality is parents do understand. Parents do understand their children better than anticipated. They are strict and overprotective of us because they understand that life is hard to figure out. Their desire is for their child to have things better than them and hope we don't make as many mistakes as they did when they were younger.

Who are your parents? Your parents are not always just your biological parents. They exist beyond biological borders and are known as extended parents. These people can be adopted or foster parents, grandparents, siblings, ministers, teachers, and coaches. All these people really do care about our wellbeing. They have paternal intentions in our lives because of what they see in us as human beings. Most of them see our true potentials to do well and realize that sometimes people just need some additional help and encouragement on life's journey. For example, a teenager may be a strong student as far as behavior in the classroom and may play basketball well, but he or she does not have the best of grades. The coach then speaks to the student about classroom work and test-taking skills. The coach tells the student to come by his office after school and gets him some tutorial services. Not only does the coach help, but he encourages the student to continue to work and strive for greatness in all things because he believes that any person can do anything if they are willing to work and sacrifice to achieve the goal set forth.

Exercise:

Name some people who influenced your life in a positive way. How did they influence your life in a positive way?

Individual's Names	How they influenced your life in a positive way?

The Real Enemy - *The Inner-Me*

Successful Thoughts:

We as people must begin to understand that we can't help others until we help ourselves first.

Being selfish about your goals, ambition, and inspirations about your life is not something to be ambiguous about, but it should be something that is of importance and accomplishment for self.

*To see more encouraging and motivational thoughts go to page **69**.*

Note: *People who take time out for you and encourage you to do well love and care about you as a human being and person.*

As children, preteens, adolescents, young adults, and adults, it is very important that we understand the value of obedience and do things that are positive. Positive behaviors will promote positive rewards. Why? Because being obedient will one day save your life or someone else's and that will increase the honor of your life and the awards afterwards. We love to be known for doing things well. It is natural because it reflects who you truly are as a person. I believe that we are all inherently kind and that doing well is an innate ability that all human beings possess. One way to identify your good nature is through meditation. Take that time for yourself, even if it is before going to sleep. This is a way to prepare for the next day and it helps us to implement our change from wrong behavior or negative things.

True honor comes when someone has done something beneficial with respect, pride, and discipline.

In today's society I hear a lot of teenagers say it is hard to do right, when there are so many distractions around. It is true things have changed, but the idea of surviving is the same. It seems that teenagers today don't care about things that have moral value. I do believe that it is not easy for young people to understand how to balance things, because a great percentage of young people are in the parental role in the absence of their parents. It is imperative that young people understand there are consequences to all of their actions. For example, as a teenager I witnessed my friend going to jail for getting into mischief like smoking, stealing, gang banging, and killing an elderly woman.

The Real Enemy - *The Inner-Me*

There are a few things that as teenagers you can do that may save you from doing things that get you into trouble, such as:

1. Being involved in church, youth programs, and mentoring programs
2. Being involved with school activities such as basketball, track or even being a little league coach
3. Working a part-time job during the week and/or on weekends
4. Volunteering with a community-based organization to help others in need
5. Doing chores and helping elders
6. Participate in youth or ongoing school or community activities
7. Opening your own business

Exercise:

Name more items that you can do to keep out of trouble or make the world a better place.

1. _____
2. _____
3. _____
4. _____
5. _____

Note: *Know that you are very valuable to the world and it is important you make decisions that will help you survive in life.*

Successful Thoughts:

We are all born to be great but greatness must be willing and able to prove it by becoming good, better and great.

Problem solving requires the TRUTH about the situation. The truth will set and make you free mentally.

If you make mistakes and you are punished for it, then you are supposed to learn from the experience as a lifelong lesson. Don't do it again!

*To see more encouraging and motivational thoughts go to page **69**.*

The Real Enemy - *The Inner-Me*

Your goals motivate your desires and drive. It will please you with relief, happiness, and peace of mind when you reach them and become the person you desire to be. Remember: no plan, no progress, and no future. To do well and be positive you must be conscientious; practice this and understand that change does not happen overnight, but over a period of time. It is my belief that everyone has greatness inside of himself or herself but to release that greatness, it requires the will to strive with the desire to be good and positive in everything. To become the best, remember to surround yourself around others who are doing well or greater than you. Practice makes perfect.

Exercise: ☞

Write down a personal statement to explain why you believe it is important to do well and be positive. How will your success please people and make others proud of you.

_____
_____
_____
_____
_____
_____
_____
_____
_____
_____
_____

◄ *No Plan, No Progress and No Future.* ►
Loving yourself first is the step to enlightenment!

Why is it so important for people to be positive and strive for even better? For self! One thing I know is that teenagers and adults need to be selfish about the things that are valuable and the things that will allow progress to transform and mold them to live successfully. Personal selfishness makes a person do things for self-satisfaction, and everyone must be willing to do things for self because when everything and everyone is gone you must be happy with yourself and the things done within each day. In order to help someone else you must first help yourself.

Never settle for just enough or what other people give you! Why? Everyone's intentions are not in your favor; know the company you keep. Everything done is based on trust and the relationship that is established. Make this a personal rule: only depend on your own abilities and listen to others' positive,

The Real Enemy - *The Inner-Me*

constructive advice. Positive, constructive advice is good, if it is meant to help you do something better or achieve something you have never achieved positively. Why is this a valid point? Sometimes we give our greatness away and then we become comfortable in accepting being second best. Don't get me wrong, training is good and you should be always willing to be trained, but you should know when the training is up. Why? After the training there should be advancement and it should happen within the time frame of a few years. The reason is simple: you have to value your self worth enough to want to advance yourself or you will accept crumbs off the table for less and wonder later why you did not get to the next level of advancement.

One of the keys to the rewards system is to perform at your best and not to let others see you sweat. Always know who to ask for help, know when to ask for help, and never appear that you have a lack of complete understanding. When you are giving your all to a situation you are developing and activating an inward determination to persevere. This should enable you to strive to achieve goals. The acknowledgement you receive is because of what you have earned with honor and hard work. You should always reassess higher goals for yourself. Work hard and practice with the intention to become an achiever and others will assist you in your transformation into a better performer. This mind state and ability will transfer into the required attitude to positively exist at work, or complete poems, or write books, but in general finish things you start.

According to the American Psychological Association's article titled, "Improving Students' Relationships with Teachers to Provide Essential Supports for Learning: Positive relationships can also help a student develop socially" (Rimm-Kaufman) positive effects stem not only from the relationships that children have with their parents. It is important to see that although well-trained teachers (and this can be extended to coaches and any other authoritative adult) should be making efforts to build rapport with students for this very reason, youth can take this responsibility into their own hands. If you would like to grow, make more positive choices, and stay on the right path seek out an adult with who you can confide in, feel comfortable saying you're confused or angry to, and bounce ideas off of. "[…] students who have close, positive and supportive relationships with their teachers will attain higher levels of achievement than those students with more conflictual relationships. If a student feels a personal connection to a teacher, experiences frequent communication with a teacher, and receives more guidance and praise than criticism from the teacher, then the student is likely to become more trustful of that teacher, show more engagement in the academic content presented, display better classroom behavior, and achieve at higher levels academically." So by making efforts to get along with your teachers, your academics will flourish. That's an amazing start to staying on the right track. The article continues to address what

The Real Enemy - *The Inner-Me*

is called the self-system theory. "Students come to the classroom with three basic psychological needs — competence, autonomy and relatedness — all of which can be met in a classroom through students' interactions with teachers and with the learning environment (Deci & Ryan, 2002). Positive teacher-student relationships help students meet these needs. Teachers offer feedback to students to support their feelings of competence. Teachers who know their students' interests and preferences and show regard and respect for these individual differences bolster students' feelings of autonomy. Teachers who establish a personal and caring relationship and foster positive social interactions within their classrooms meet their students' needs for relatedness (or social connection to school)." It makes sense for a teenager transitioning into adulthood to want to be a success. If studies suggest the relationships you establish with your teachers will promote growth and success, then make sure you work to maintain a benevolent relationship. Participate positively, help others in the classroom, communicate clearly, and be truthful. These are all things that help you to help yourself.

Exercise: 👉

Below write down some sayings or quotes that people said to you or provided to you over the years. Reflect on how those sayings or quotes encouraged you through life.

What was the saying or quote?	By Whom?	What impact positive impact did it have on your life?	When did they say it to you?

The Real Enemy - *The Inner-Me*

> **Successful Thoughts:**
>
> Renewing and reeducate yourself from mental slavery and no one can free you but YOU.
>
> Mental entrapment is the lack of ability to let pain, hurt and the lack of love go.
>
> No one is immune to the errors and trials in this life. If you fall down, then get up and try again until you get it right.
>
> *To see more encouraging and motivational thoughts go to page **69**.*

━ *Believing In Yourself* ━

I know this may sound selfish and egotistic (and it is), but if you don't believe in yourself enough to live a life full of love and happiness, then who will? No one! Don't expect to find happiness through things and other people. Discover who you are and love yourself because you are alive. Everyone has to have confidence in self. It takes selfish acts to create acts of selfishness for others.

In other words, you have to achieve your goals first in order to help someone else with their goals. The attitude necessary for saving your own life is to live within the lesson learned by living. With that in mind remember to always continue to build yourself through education, life experiences, and achievements. This is how you build a worthwhile reputation with influential power. People today, and in the past, like to be around people with respect and status. Status encourages the individual to continue to do benevolent things and with a positive reputation there are sometimes special privileges and rewards. Don't talk about it. Be about it first and talk later. There are a lot of people who talk up a good game but can't produce any results, and they find excuses to justify why they are not doing it or why someone else won't let them do it. Jealousy and envy is a thief that kills and destroys a good reputation. People may be envious because they are LAZY and don't want to change. They are haters with a dark side because they can't do. It is easier to talk about someone else than to do for yourself. Never let anyone talk you down because of the things you do well. Their talk can be your downfall if you listen to negative people, and that is why it is important to surround yourself with positive people who are doing what you trying to do.

The Real Enemy - *The Inner-Me*

Exercise: 👉

Finding yourself is the hardest thing to do but realizing what you enjoy doing is not. There are things in life that puts a smile on your face or just relaxes you. Everyone has things that they enjoy doing.

What are your favorite books that you have read and you keep reading them over and over again?
_____
_____
_____
_____

What are your favorite hobbies, sports and arts and crafts that relax you and keep you smiling every time you start one? You don't stop until you are finished.
_____
_____
_____
_____
_____

Travelling brings joy to many because they get to go to places they never been before. Travelling is like exploring and finding something new in life. Do you like travelling? Where do you like to go? How do you like to travel?
_____
_____
_____
_____
_____

Successful Thoughts:

I am on my way. I may not know my final destination; however, I have had a preview and now I know I'm bound for greatness because
I AM SOMEBODY.

Change your perception, change your behavior, and change your understanding about life. Nothing is impossible!

*To see more encouraging and motivational thoughts go to page **69**.*

The Real Enemy - *The Inner-Me*

Obedience and honor is a reward you owe to yourself, family, and others who care about your wellbeing because they care and love you. Imagine you're an athlete and you want to be the best on the team, but your coach notices that every time you get the chance to prove that you are the best, you make a mistake and then lose your cool and control by stomping and yelling aloud. The coach calls you into the office to talk to you about your performance. He or she starts out by saying what a great athlete you are and how you are one of the best, if not the best player on the team, and he encourages you to focus more on correcting your mistakes because in a real game situation it can cost the team a disqualification and valuable points.

>The coach says, "We all have made mistakes and you will make mistakes too but through practice and following the coaches lead it won't be so hard."

So you look at the coach and say, "Why is that?"

The coach says, "To know the mistake, to correct the mistake, and to eliminate the mistake." Practice, practice, and more practice will help create and make winners. No one is immune to mistakes!

We are imperfect people and have made many mistakes and without the mistakes we would not know what to look for the next time it happens. It has been said it is better to listen to others' advice and guidance rather than making mistakes. This is easier said than done, but it requires discipline and trust. Trust is hard especially when you have trusted and it was broken. You were taken advantage of for no reason. That is why it is important to trust yourself first, ask for help, watch, and listen to know if a person is in your corner or not. Trust is not given; it is earned.

Here are seven suggestions for how to build trust with yourself and anyone in your life:

    1. Identify a mentor, ask questions, and listen to the answer. Remember the answer (take notes) because the objective is to improve yourself and to trust someone else.

    2. Research the answers to build yourself up and if you have questions, ask for clarity.

    3. Do something good for the mentor. Giving is a sign of gratitude and a way to say, "Thank you."

    4. Create a situation where their opinion is needed to help with a situation. Listen to the advice and this will help you become a better listener. If the response is positive then it most likely is good advice.

    5. Communicate what you feel or dislike. This will encourage dialogue to gain a better understanding in order to add to what you already know.

The Real Enemy - *The Inner-Me*

6. Understand that what you are learning and doing is something that you should want to do for others. Life is about helping those who ask you for it.
7. True trust is received and given from both persons.

If you feel good about this person remember friends must go through ups and downs. Trust is the will to endure and remember before giving up on someone. Trust allows you to communicate and give that person a chance to correct or apologize for the situation. Training others to Respect who you are as a person and not to be Used by others or Someone who is unworthy to be Trusted by your friendship (T.R.U.S.T.).

Successful Thoughts:

Speak life and love over yourself and it will happen as long as you practice it daily with an awareness to manifest it.

One way to identify your good nature is through meditation. Take that time for yourself.

There is a cost for life and love. Nothing is free.

*To see more encouraging and motivational thoughts go to page **69**.*

Here are six helpers that demonstrate the attitude everyone must have to change and make a difference in their own lives for the benefit of things. It does not make a difference what the situation is that you are going through; there is always a beneficial and positive answer to the problem. Remember these six helpers:

Helper	Statement
Helper One	You will always need a parent, coach, or teacher to teach you and help you stay focused, committed, and disciplined to achieve your goal.
Helper Two	You must have the desire to want the best for yourself and be able to prove it in your performances.
Helper Three	Practice and strive to reach your goals daily, weekly, and annually and know that there will be mistakes. There will be things you don't know or did not see coming. Get up, ask for help, and do it again better.
Helper Four	Don't give up. Always complete what you start. Persevere in all things.
Helper Five	Always strive to be the best in every positive thing you do and don't let negative people tell you what you can or can't do. Give 100% in everything you do and it will pay off when you least expect it. You never know who is watching.
Helper Six	A good attitude is everything, and it will take you a long way.

The Real Enemy - *The Inner-Me*

Remember: It is worthwhile to have people in your life that will help motivate and inspire you to stay focused. Staying focused requires you to strive to reach your goals successfully.

Successful Thoughts:

An opportunist seeks the chance to do and strives with their mind to create their life with greater possibilities.

We are not alone in life, rely on someone who can help.

Stop, look and listen before your respond with a negative word, ask for clarity.

*To see more encouraging and motivational thoughts go to page **69.***

Chapter 3

Abide
Follow the Rules

The Real Enemy - *The Inner-Me*

Chapter 3

Abide
Follow the Rules

It is understood that the law of parents and the state law are one and the same in principle. The two share the same purpose, which is to serve and protect the innocent. In the eyes of parents and the state, each child or children are innocent until proven guilty and that is why it is very important that everyone in the community abide and not break the law.

Parents will make statements like, "This is my house and as long as you live here you will abide by my rules and regulations," and if you are disobedient you will be given a punishment. The same is true with the law.

Exercise: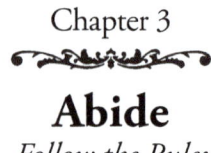

Take the time to think about the rules of the house. How did they help you in the real world? What character trait did they build?

Trait	House Rule	How did the rule impact you in a positive way?

Successful Thoughts:

Ruling self is the first rule of achievement for self.

In all situation challenges blame self or look at self to determine as an individual what could I have done differently 1st and 2nd talk to each other about the experience to determine how to fix the situation to establish a common understanding and because love and understanding is objective result we want.

*To see more encouraging and motivational thoughts go to page **69**.*

The Real Enemy - *The Inner-Me*

If you break the law and go to juvenile detention or jail, the police officer will say, "This is your new home and we have rules here that you must obey and if you break the rules you will be in the hole for a week."

Punishment with parents or the law is one and the same and the reason why punishment is so important. Punishments reinforce good behavior and attempt to eliminate bad character traits. The whole idea of good and bad is to ensure that people feel safe and secure. So if you listen to your parents and extended parents you should survive in society and live a nice, safe life, but if you don't there are consequences for your actions within the law.

There are two types of consequences: rewards and punishments.

An example of a good and rewarding consequence occurs when a person has done well. They are recognized or rewarded for it. For example, if you bring home five A's and two B's on your report card and you get $5 per A and $2 per B. Because of the financial incentive you are energized and persuaded to strive to bring in more A's than B's because you can receive $35 instead of $29.

An example of a bad or punishable consequence involves a person who has done something unacceptable or wrong and is punished for it. For example, your parent(s) talks to you about stealing and how it is not good to steal but one day you are out with friends and everyone has money to by some snacks and a soda, but you. You feel embarrassed to ask someone to buy you something.
Instead, as everyone is walking toward the line to pay for the items, you decide to place the items in your pocket, but as you leave an adult sees you. The store manager warns you and knows your parent(s) and will call your house. By the time you return home your parent(s) are there and ask you about it and you lie. You are put on punishment for a month for stealing and lying. You are informed that you will not receive any allowance but instead you must write a paper on the law of stealing and its consequence. Understand that parents are designed to teach you the importance of life and its long lesson. It is their desire that you do well in life and their hope is that you never go jail to learn this lesson.

━ Parental Law ━

Parental laws are the rules that help you survive as a child until you become an adult. Parental laws are designed to teach each individual how to conduct themselves at home, school, church, and in public. Believe it or not, these rules are designed to have an impact on your adult life once you leave home for college, military, a job, or anything on your own.

The Real Enemy - *The Inner-Me*

Parental laws are in place to serve and protect you as a child and once you become a productive citizen, you will have the foundation to survive.

⎯ The Law ⎯

The law is the binding practice of a community to rule and protect all individuals. If broken, there are laws to help reinforce controlling acts by authority to protect the citizens and the whole community from individual who are wrong and in violation of the law.

Comparison of parental law and the law:

> Both are designed to serve and protect.
> Both have consequences and punishment.
> Both are designed to teach a lesson.
> Both are designed to create positive behavior.
> Both are designed to have us do the right thing.

Contrast of parental law and the law:
> Parental law has short-term punishment (weeks or a month).
> Parental laws give us another chance without a strike against us in society.
> Parental laws are filled with love grace and determination for change with freedom.
> Parental laws are broken too many times (e.g. you will be put out of your parent(s) house).
> The law has short-term and long-term punishment (years).
> The law gives a second chance with a record by your name.
> The laws reinforced by strict and sometimes brutal determination for change without freedom.
> The law, if broken again, will get you a long sentence in jail.
>
> It is imperative that all children and adults understand parental laws and the law to survive in society.

Food for thought:
There are two places for people who do not conform and comply with either law: prison or the grave. Therefore, it is important to listen and abide by the laws and do well in life to discover your true potential and abilities with prosperity.

The Real Enemy - *The Inner-Me*

> **Successful Thoughts:**
>
> Stop with given into negative thoughts and do something positive
>
> Dream are nothing without learning and implementation for it to become the reality.
>
> *To see more encouraging and motivational thoughts go to page **69**.*

Exercise: 👉

It is very important that everyone living understand the importance of becoming a law abiding citizen.

Write down the importance of abiding by both the parental law and the law:

_____
_____
_____
_____
_____
_____
_____

What is the purpose and goal of obeying the both law?

_____
_____
_____
_____
_____
_____
_____
_____

The Real Enemy - *The Inner-Me*

Based on what you know about laws and the purpose of them, write down what will happen to people who break the law.

_____
_____
_____
_____
_____
_____
_____
_____

Successful Thoughts:

Agree with your challenges quickly! Why! To resolve it and move on to next level of doing things.

Being alive is not enough to understand the importance of becoming a contributor with an intent.

*To see more encouraging and motivational thoughts go to page **69**.*

Chapter 4

Discovery
Know thyself

Chapter 4

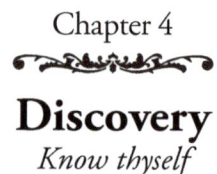

Discovery
Know thyself

An old African proverb says, "Know thyself." This statement is so powerful when you understand the content of the words. My intention is to break down the understanding of this passage in a simple form for a better understanding with substance and purpose.

Who are you? You are a body of elements that make up a human being, regardless of pigmentation and ethnic background. We are all born with a uniqueness that separates all from one another. Discovering yourself is (or should be) more important to you than anyone else, but you do need others to help you bring out your full potential. We all have something to offer the world and the people in it, but we must be in line to receive it and to reach it. What is it? It is the understanding of life and discovering your purpose. The only way you can know is by living. If you don't experience life to the fullness of its goodness, then you have not begun to live.

Understand this! If you make mistakes and you are punished for it, then you are supposed to learn from the experience as a lifelong lesson. Don't do it again, but if you keep making them over and over again, the next time you may get into deeper trouble that can harm your life.

Exercise: 👉

Think about some mistakes you made in life. What did you learn from those mistakes?

Mistakes	What positive thing did you learn from those mistakes?	How did the lesson from those mistakes change your life?

The Real Enemy - *The Inner-Me*

Note: *Every lesson in life teaches and empowers all of us to do better and punishments are to inform all of us that it is wrong and to stop doing it before it is too late.*

Successful Thoughts:

The awaken of love is like setting goals, you have to achieve the success

Discovery you purpose in life is worth the journey you will experience and the accomplishments you will achieve.

What you give is what you will receive but how good and pleasant it is will be determined by you attitude and intention.

*To see more encouraging and motivational thoughts go to page **69**.*

What this means is the decisions you make today will greatly impact your future, and only you can decide which direction to go by the choices you make.

Know yourself and prove to yourself that you can do anything when you put your mind to it, and everyone else will see it too. If you don't have anything to prove, then you are not living within the circle of life.
How do I know myself? Below is a list of things that describe who we are as people and I will make mention of some Biblical points.

- God, or the Creator, created you to be good (Genesis Chapter 1 of King James version) and God created both you and your parents to be good.
- You were created and conceived from your parents uniquely.
- You are good in all things and you have a chance to be better at your will.
- Remember your innocence, dreams, desires, and what you wanted to do since you were younger.
- The things you would do for free is part of who you are and what you are to do.
- Listen to positive people who encourage you because they will give their best advice for what they think you should be working on for a career.
- Know that life is not perfect and we all have a chance to correct some wrongs. Strive to do things that are good and encouraging to self and for others.

To be the best you must know who you are, what your goals are in life, strive through practice, and always ask for help and training to reach your full potential and success.

The Real Enemy - *The Inner-Me*

Exercise: 👉

How is your life segmented for success? Write the different activities, goals or accomplishments that you have in progress or you are thinking about putting into place. Each one of these items is a stepping stone to success.

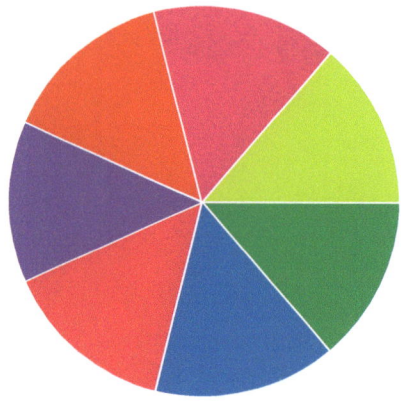

Successful Thoughts:

We are all gifted but we must invest in developing our talents to be effective in using the gift.

Leadership is and innate and develop ability but your have to invest in understanding the concepts, philosophies and principals of being an effective leader.

Think strategically and it will raise your awareness and support to be able to master the task.

*To see more encouraging and motivational thoughts go to page **69**.*

To be good is not just saying it, it is the ability to prove it to others. Good is not self-proclaiming but only exists when others witness your achievements.

To be good is the objective for everything in life. For example, you make a mistake and the lesson learned is to correct the mistake by doing it right, good, or better the next time. Good is a natural state of being! It is bad that is unnatural! Bad is so unnatural that it can turn into a disease or it can be an opportunity to transform. It is your viewpoint.

The Real Enemy - *The Inner-Me*

Mental Notes: An opportunist seeks the chance to do and strives with their mind to create their life with greater possibilities.

Boys to Men and Girls to Women
This is a transition you will experience one day. Once you have decided to put away childish things and acknowledge your responsibilities as an independent person, you then must grow strong in your faith and put your life into actions for success.

It is so important that you accept roles of leadership and be a strong and disciplined follower at the same time. To achieve any goal in this life you must first have and understand honesty, discipline, commitment and dedication. These are the foundational tools for success. Set your goals high and operate with faith. Believe in yourself until it is accomplished internally and you can duplicate it externally.

Exercise: ☞

Look at the chart to see what type of leader you would like to be. Then look at the chart to see what type of leader you really are. Think about the ideal leader and how do you make it to that leader. What do you need to change about yourself? Note: When you think about personality traits you often think about habits or actions of a person. A personality trait is a distinguishing characteristic or quality of a person from a trend of their actions, outlooks, feelings, and habits on specific things, situations or people. Examples of traits: Accessible, Active, Adaptable, Charming, Cheerful, Faithful, etc.

List the traits that you would like to have:
_____
_____
_____

List the traits that you carry:
_____
_____
_____

Once you have reviewed the chart look at some of the traits that you must have to become the leader you desire to become. List up to five traits that you need to have to become the desired leader and develop a plan on how you can become that leader. Also note in the space below the chart on how long will it take for you to develop such a trait.

The Real Enemy - *The Inner-Me*

Leadership Chart			
Leadership Theories	Strengths:	Weaknesses:	Personal Reaction
Path-Goal Theory	Using a Path Goal Theory approach to leadership has several positive features. Firstly, this theory attempts to incorporate the motivation principles of the expectancy theory and second its model is practical and easy to use.	Although there are several positive aspect of Path-Goal Theory, it fail to explain the different roles of leaders and managers. The time constraints to effectively deploys very narrow.	Although in an attempt to clearly visualize the vision, I sometimes get caught up in the overall progress and save little time to consider the individual.
Implication for :			
Self	Team	Organization	Culture
In order to employ this approach effectively, it would be helpful to create a questionnaire for staff, in order to uncover some of their motivators. Communication between myself and team members is vital for success.	Teams are strong because they know what the goal is and have a clear roadmap to accomplish the mission.	The theory allows for building. Teams goals become departmental goals, departmental goals become organizational goals. For the organization this theory helps push forward organizational initiatives.	The culture of the organization when using the path-goal theory suggest that motivation of employees is a strategic direction, and is a used as a method for production.

Leadership Chart			
Leadership Theories	Strengths:	Weaknesses:	Personal Reaction
Situational Theory	Situational leadership provides a straightforward approach and is easily used. Another strength of this approach, is the fact that it teaches leaders flexibility.	Situational leadership has been criticized for several reasons, one the lack of evidence in its reliability. Second, it does not fully address interaction of groups verse individuals.	The situation approach has flexibility and allows leaders to place individuals into a work flow where they will accomplish the most, or be most productive.
Implication for :			
Self	Team	Organization	Culture
In order for this approach to be most successful I must conduct a task analysis in order to be sure that all of the events necessary to produce have been accounted for prior to setting up the team members.	In general the team will have a feeling that everyone has a part and is contributing to the assigned mission. Team motivation can be developed when all ream members feel successful and are good at the task.	At an organizational level, the situational approach allows for change and flexibility. This approach looks at the task at hand and produces the qualified resources to accommodate it.	The culture of the organization seems to be accommodating and supporting, they don't set their employees up for failure.

The Real Enemy - *The Inner-Me*

Leadership Chart			
Leadership Theories	Strengths:	Weaknesses:	Personal Reaction
Transformational Theory	Transformational leadership theory provides a broader view of leadership, it places a strong emphasis on followers needs, values and morals.	Some suggest that this approach traits leadership as a personality trait rather that a behavior. It is also unclear as to whether or not this leader is a visionary.	I am able to communicate the positive and the negative about implementing new technologies. I offer to staff the reasons why we need to change and how it will effect them.
Implication for :			
Self	Team	Organization	Culture
This approach is one I use often, in order to gain the respect of others you need to value them and their thoughts as well. Communication is a key tool for using this approach.	Open communication between leaders, team members and staff are utilized with this approach. Acceptance of ideas from team members occurs during the decision making process.	Teams, team members, departments and all staff alike feel as though they are part of the decision making during change.	The organization is lead by someone staff trust, he/she has buy-in from stakeholders.

List the five to ten leadership traits from desired leadership style:

_____
_____
_____
_____

List the traits and your development plan for that specific trait:

_____
_____
_____
_____

The Real Enemy - *The Inner-Me*

Mental Notes: *Life is not fair all the time. There are many disappointments you will encounter along the way but if you are fair in all your ways, then life will bless you the same.*

No one is immune to the errors and trials in this life. If you fall down, then get up and try again until you get it right.

Successful Thoughts:

I am who I visualize, speak into existence and believe I am.

Your hope and aspiration is your drive to be unique and become greater than your circumstance of tomorrow.

If you don't see pain as character builder and see the challenges as opportunities you will always misread and misunderstand the action of the terms overcome, perseverance and achievements.

*To see more encouraging and motivational thoughts go to page **69.***

Chapter 5

Your Roots

Remember to come back to the middle.

Chapter 5

Your Roots
Remember to come back to the middle.

There are three levels in the game of life: the beginning, the middle, and the end. As difficult times come, always go back to the middle.

What is the middle? Why is the middle so important?

The middle is the basic foundation of understanding for all human beings. The middle is understanding, respect, discipline, perseverance, and love. The middle is the place of silence, meditation, and creative visualization. The middle is the place we go to collect our thoughts and reevaluate ourselves and our personal plans.

As children, teenagers, and adults we often find ourselves in hard situations that are sometimes overwhelming to us. We may feel like going off on someone or something. That is the time you must go and take about five to ten minutes to vent away from everyone else and the situation at hand. Go walking or speak to someone you can confide in without biased opinions. The middle is a place for you to leave everything and channel your thoughts on situations that will not incriminate your or hinder your future endeavors with emotional reactions.

The middle is the ability to communicate and express how you feel (e.g., good, sad, mad, angry, etc.) without harming yourself or others. For example, when you are feeling as if everything is going wrong in your life and things are not moving logically or as planned, instead of getting upset and yelling at someone or going out and getting a drink, take some smooth soft relaxing music and play it low for only your ear to hear. Then take ten deep inhales and exhales. Imagine an ocean with sunrays beaming on your face and smile. Repeat this at least for five to ten minutes (depending on your relief). These types of solutions are more beneficial than allowing something that would cause detriment.

Some people believe the Almighty Creator can only save us from life's disparities, but the truth of this is quoted in the Bible: "Knock and it shall be opened, ask and you shall receive." You walk alone and the Creator will walk with you until you finish your path. We are all born with all power and that is from the Creator but we must learn to use the power of choice and will to do good or evil. The Creator has given us the power but we depend on God to do everything for us and not ourselves. Doing well and being positive is always the best choice.

The Real Enemy - *The Inner-Me*

At this point, the middle is peace of mind, oneness with self, and receiving insightful and inspiring information to help you move on in your journey. Remember the experiences you encounter daily are for you to hear and see. Only those who seek to know and understand will live and evolve.

Exercise: 👉

Think about some mistakes you made and how you got out of it. Write down at least three mistake, who did you call for help and what was their advice to you to help?

1._____

2._____

3._____

Successful Thoughts:

No man comes from himself and can't create anything from nothing.

There is never a perfect timing to live your dreams or accomplish your goal or making a difference in life to make an impact. The perfect timing is always RIGHT NOW, TODAY!

You have the power to make the opportunity available but you have to strive and endure all life adversity and stay focus on your goal.

*To see more encouraging and motivational thoughts go to page **69**.*

Chapter 6

The Battle
The Enemy is my Inner-Self

The Real Enemy - *The Inner-Me*

Chapter 6

The Battle
The Enemy is my Inner-Self.

The illusive illusion is realizing what real is, where reality is, and who it is about.
The power of the mind is as small or as large as we know and conceptualize.

Who are you?
What is life about?
Why do you feel discouraged at times?
How do I overcome my challenges?
These questions are answered NOW. Read on!

Life is about continuous strength to survive with the will of determination to move forward positively through all adversities. Only the strong will be victorious, and the race of life is not given to anyone. For example, there once was a little boy who dreamed about becoming a great air pilot and at night he would pray that one day his dream would come true. As the child grew and reached the age of 15, he had a dream of flying an airplane and that night, before he went to bed he prayed, "God, one day I want to be a great airplane pilot and I want to be the best at flying."

At 18 years of age he was preparing for his graduation day. One day he and his friends went to a palm reader's shop to know what their future holds.
When it was his turn the old fortuneteller said to him, "You know your future, so why are you here?"
He stated, "No one knows their future and the things that will happen."
The teller said," Very well. I see you falling from the sky and you probably should not ride on planes because something will happen."
He said, "What will happen?"
She said, "That's all I know. The rest is up to you."

Ten years passed and the same young man was afraid of flying. As a career choice, he became a business consultant and only took road trips, but one night he fell asleep and dreamed of falling from the sky. He woke-up in a cold sweat. Then one day his father came to visit him and asked if he was happy with his lifestyle and if he was pursuing his goals.

The Real Enemy - *The Inner-Me*

His father said, "It is strange that you are a businessman and not a pilot, because you have always dreamed of flying planes and becoming the best pilot."

The son said, "That was only a dream and not reality."

Five years later, the young man got a phone call from his mother and she informed him that his father had passed and there is a will to be read.

A week later and after the funeral, the young man attended the reading of his father's will and it stated, "My dear and only beloved son, I love you with all my heart and soul. I have tried to raise you to the best of my ability and give both you and your mother the best, with all that I had to give. I need you to know that life is very unpredictable. Sometimes things are not what they may seem to be. I leave with you these keys and a paid registration for pilot classes. After completing the classes, contact Mr. Hope and he will show you your airplane."

Five years had passed since the reading of his father's will and the young man was still having the bad dreams. One day he finally realized that he wanted to pursue his lifelong dream despite the nightmare and the fortuneteller's warning. He attended the pilot classes and he called Mr. Hope. Mr. Hope gave him the keys and showed him the planes his father had purchased and informed him that these were the best planes around the world. His father had purchased five large, private 75-seat passenger planes, left a 25-year running business, the plan and projection, and the business registration titles and deeds in his name to continue operations as the owner and president.

The young man asked Mr. Hope, "How and with what money?"

Mr. Hope said, "Your father worked hard and saved a lot. He always said that you would be the best pilot and businessman that the world would ever saw."

Successful Thoughts:

Total affirmation cancel out by the overwhelming power of the act of fundamental contradictions, the TRUTH.

If you are going to fight for your life, then fight harder than the next man, because he is fighting too.

*To see more encouraging and motivational thoughts go to page **69**.*

The Real Enemy - *The Inner-Me*

The Enemy "The Battle Within"

An unstable mind turns against itself and is its own worst enemy.

> "Through training, the student becomes transformed. Self-importance, vanity, false pride, all fear-based behaviors, are replaced by positive attributes such as humility, calmness and inner peace. The higher-self always wants to be known, and positive change and transcendence are always available"
> - Vesia.

The battle begins the very first time we rebel against our parents, teachers or other authoritative figures in our lives. This is the beginning of many problems we bring on ourselves. That is why it is important that as children and teenagers we learn to follow the rules of the house and abide by the law of the land. The battle is a normal place that people experience in their lives. The battle is another way of saying challenges the mind encounters when having to making choices. The challenges are either good and bad, right and wrong, or obedience and disobedience, and will determine the battle. These are your actions and how you make decisions. As we grow up we learned that certain things can earn award(s) and that is the mind state we all need to survive. It is an understanding that doing well can reap benefits that add to your character and credits your actions and the benefit of making decisions.

Transferable Behavior:
Adolescent Years

Believe it or not, how you behave as an adolescent and teenager will transfer into your adulthood life until you make some serious, conscious changes. For example, as children and teenagers our parent(s) told us, you don't have to lie about anything and you could ask them any question. Instead, we lied. We all have done this at one time or another, but some learned not to continue lying and others continue to lie, which has or have transferred over into our teenage years or adulthood. This type of behavior will only lead to more lies, stealing, robbery, killing, jail or death.

As adolescents and teenagers it is very important that you value your life enough not to allow negative behavior or people influence you to the point that they control you. What do I mean? Don't let anyone control you! We are all

The Real Enemy - *The Inner-Me*

influenced by other people's words, opinions, and behaviors whether they are good or bad. That is the human nature in us all, but at some point in life we must become wiser and learn to think and make certain decisions that benefit us in a positive manner. Believe me, I understand many children are being raised in one-parent households and if they have never been corrected for the behavior as a child, then it will seem a challenge or sometimes a conflict of interest. In life you will be corrected on the things that you do wrong and the reason for the correction is to learn not to do that particular behavior again. In short, the faster you learn to make good choices and that doing the right things, the less trouble you will endure twice.

Exercise: ☞

Write down some positive phrases that you should be telling yourself everyday…

_____
_____
_____
_____

Successful Thoughts:

There are situation in life that will be used to bend and pressure your character to pull out your will of self-control and maturity.

All test are designed for everyone to pass and move to the next level.

*To see more encouraging and motivational thoughts go to page **69**.*

Chapter 7

Mental Entrapment

Chapter 7

Mental Entrapment

If you accept and allow negative statements, thoughts, and stereotypes to consume your thoughts and behaviors, then you cannot break the chains of oppression and self-destruction until you change your perception of life.

Mental Entrapment is not an innate ability or something you are born with; it is a learned behavior through negative exposure. Mental entrapment is when you are not sure about self, life, and what you should be doing for yourself. It is sometimes created within the culture of your surrounding. Mental entrapment is a self-destructive act. In short, mental entrapment is the lack of ability to tell the truth. Admit the truth and accept the truth about self, others, and situations.

The mind is full of optical illusions and that is how we sometimes interpret life's situations. We tend to only see things in the now and not the failure or glory of the situation, and because we are taught only to see the pain, we embed painful memories and our perception is deemed bleak and shady. This only one conditional train of thought and this type of thinking is dangerous to the whole human race. Why? Because it creates a negative thinking process and behavior that can become condemnation for self and others. It also can create a negativity that can slowly increase negative self-behavior that could lead to sickness, decrease hope, and the possibility of good things happening which includes good people entering your life that may be able to help and assist your life.

This negative thinking process can appear in the form of revenge, depression, oppression, violence, avoidance, envy, and self-abuse. These types of negative thoughts create a negative character whose behaviors can be dangerous to self and others. This thought process is self-destruction and will soon cause an elimination of self-image, self-esteem, and cause a distance of family or friends. It could also lead to drug use and isolation from society that could lead to homelessness, jail, or to the grave. This is a critical process that is killing our youth, family, and friends.

Self-destruction is indirect reflection about how you view yourself both inwardly and outwardly. Low self-esteem is the lack of confidence in self and everyone needs a high self-esteem to compete in all areas and aspects of life both personal and professional. Low self-esteem destructs the ability and desire to want to do well and could lead to serious mental and physical problems. Self-destruction is mental entrapment.

The Real Enemy - *The Inner-Me*

Exercise: 👉

Write the Opposite of the words in box below:

Negative Words	Positive Words	Definition of Positive Words
Revenge		
Depression		
Oppression		
Violence		
Avoidance		
Envy		
Self-Abuse		
Self-Destruction		

Successful Thoughts:

I want to live so bad that I will do things to stay positive, seek opportunities for self-development and advance within leadership and receive all my earned rewards.

In all things have positive intention and you will have a positive outcome.

*To see more encouraging and motivational thoughts go to page **69**.*

Mental entrapment is when you can't let go of the past experience that has caused a negative outlook. A negative perception about it could hinder professional advancements within your career. The world is full of negative elements and people, but guess what? It is what it is and there is no perfection in anything or anyone.

Our past conditions are situations, but it does not determine the future successes and outcomes. All things happened in the past to prepare for future action to help someone else.

Although life does deal bad hands, it is imperative that we as mutual minds understand that we have to power of choice. Once you understand that life is based on the POWER

The Real Enemy - *The Inner-Me*

of CHOICE, then understanding, learning, and wisdom begins to create a desire to find yourself to become in tune with self, others, and spirituality. It is not meant for people to feel bondage, but life is for people to realize and reach their potentials to fulfill a purpose and reach their destinies. Know this - what you think of yourself both inwardly and outwardly will reflect in your behavior. We are all born to be great but greatness must be willing and able to prove it by becoming good, better, and great. Life is nothing more than a competitive race for jobs, careers, and retirement, and the winner will be the best performer who trained and prepared to be the best. There are some things that should be considered while training; they are personal choices. You have to plan and save; you have to have a will to learn and be self-driven as an individual. This is one way of looking at self. Another is to remember as children and adolescents we are taught in arithmetic class how to solve problems to get the correct answers. In this same way when problems, issues, and situation occur it is not for us to deny, ignore, or run away from the situation, but is for us to solve the problem. Problem solving requires the TRUTH about the situation. The truth will set and make you free mentally.

Exercise: ☞

Think of these things:

Career Choice:
_____
_____

Retirement (How old will you be? Where will you retire?)
_____
_____

How will you achieve both of these things?

Career Choice:
_____
_____

Retirement (Save for retirement -How old will you be? Where will you retire?):
_____
_____
_____

How much do you think you need for retirement? _____
How much do you have to save a year to reach your goal?
_____

The Real Enemy - *The Inner-Me*

Steps to take for retirement:
1. _____
2. _____
3. _____
4. _____
5. _____
6. _____
7. _____
8. _____
9. _____
10. _____

Successful Thoughts:

All men are created equal and others are more determine to have more than others to become the exceptional man.

What are you willing to sacrifice to gain what is good for your life?

*To see more encouraging and motivational thoughts go to page **69**.*

━ Selfish Acts ━

Generations upon generations have been taught that being selfish is wrong and a behavior that we should change. This is true and it is misunderstood at the same time. For example, being selfish about sharing with others to help them is a selfish act that could be perceived to be wrong. We should all be selfish when it come to our personal wellbeing, lifestyle, and future. It is true that no one will take care of self better than self. In most of our lives we have been taught to be givers and not takers and that we have to earn the respect of others. This is a situational truth and it is very important to know when and when not to be self.

When it comes to your wellbeing and life it is great to be selfish, because when it comes to yourself no one will ever be able to accomplish anything for you. Others can help out but no one can accomplish your personal success. When you understand that you must come first when it pertains to matters of your best interest for your life.

The Real Enemy - *The Inner-Me*

Self-acts to consider that are GREAT for your life:
1. Honor your parents, foster care parents, adoption parent and family (as long as they are positive and have your best interest in mind).
2. Graduate from high school.
3. Attend college, military, trade school, certification training for business, and complete it.
4. Attend graduate school or beyond to receive a PH.D degree.
5. Obtain and keep a job, career, or open a business. Maintain it for at least five years.
6. Meet a mate and date, practice abstinence, and (if you have sex) use sexual protections until you get married. Discuss life goals, saving, and investments.
7. Get married and plan for the next 3-5 years (living area, cars, and travel) and plan children.
8. Plan your retirement.

Successful Thoughts:

Money is an expensive habit if it is wasted, but money can be a game changer if you invest in profitable stock.

One of most interesting and enormously important person is you. Act like it.

Your plan will never bore too much fruit during your lifetime.

*To see more encouraging and motivational thoughts go to page **69**.*

How does this impact your life? If you don't plan your own life then others will have a plan for you and it may not have anything to do with your will or destiny. "Know thyself" is an old African Proverb that suggests that you should know yourself as a principle in order to survive, do anything, or help someone else out. Being selfish when it comes to your life is a positive mind state to help yourself. We as people must begin to understand that we can't help others until we help ourselves first. Helping ourselves to reach our goals is the first step to a positive selfish act. It requires that you be goal orientated, focused, determined, and passionate about living a life of happiness to be able to help someone else.

It is imperative to work on self and establish yourself first as an individual. Why? Because it will allow the opportunity for positive and like minds to become attractive

The Real Enemy - *The Inner-Me*

and connect with you, because you are out and about accomplishing and doing something as a contributor. Positive thoughts and behavior attracts positive like-minded people who are looking for others.

Being selfish about your goals, ambition, and inspirations about your life is not something to be ambiguous about, but it should be something that is of importance and accomplishment for self. Being able to make decisions about your life is essential and imperative to self and you should be careful about who you allow in your personal circle.

Exercise Example:

Simple Goal Setting Format

Name _____ Date _____

Here is what I want to achieve:

Steps to meet my goal:
1.
2.
3.
4.
5.

Here is how I am going to measure my achievement:

_____
_____
_____
_____
_____
_____
_____
_____

The Real Enemy - *The Inner-Me*

This is how I am going to celebrate once I achieve my goal:

_____
_____
_____
_____
_____

> **Successful Thoughts:**
>
> See the future. I had to win.
>
> A self-driven person is most like to make it in life with the will to learn from others.
>
> *To see more encouraging and motivational thoughts go to page **69**.*

Your personal circle of friends should be people who have your best interest and you have their best interest too. Friendship is sometimes meant for a short period of time and some are to be in your life for the long term. Everyone will not stay in your circle of friends, and then some people must be eliminated because of their intention and the harm they cause to the friendship. A street statement that I like is, "Prepare for the dumb stuff." When you see, hear, and feel those foolish people doing dumb things, let them go and just be respectful and move in life. It is very important that you learn to respect some people and let them go. Letting go is because you care and love yourself. If you don't let go you will allow and create an experience that will entrap you and attract others with the same behavior and intention, and next thing that happens is that all your so-called "friends" are causing your hurt and enjoy doing dumb stuff.

This type of behavior is one who is out of control and if you accept their expected behavior and treatment it will kill your esteem, growth, and cause a prolonging in your blessing for a better lifestyle with happiness and love. If you don't stand for your rights and respect you will fall for anything and anyone in your life. You must have standards and principals to live by to govern and honor your life. If you respect yourself then don't accept anyone who disrespects you. Don't be a hero. Heroes try to save others when they won't save themselves! No one can save another person but you can encourage them with the idea about change and the benefit of change from a state of mind. Change is the only consistent thing

The Real Enemy - *The Inner-Me*

and in life. We all as individuals have to decide what we want in life. You only can change yourself and others have to change for themselves too. It is not our responsibility to change someone else. It is hard enough just changing ourselves. Good friends usually hold onto others who don't want to change. I call this "the hero's concept."

A hero's concept is a common behavior that most people have when it comes to help, assisting, and doing for others. This is a great concept when it comes to helping others but it can be a hindrance and a handicap. It could cause the person being helped to become co-dependent. Co-dependence can be a negative character trait. How? It could lead to denial, low-esteem, and a lack of control.

Famous psychologist Abraham Maslow is responsible for the infamous Maslow's Hierarchy of Needs, which depicts a human's various motivations. It suggests that a person strives to meet basic needs and once they are met, continues on to the next set of needs. A pyramid is figuratively scaled in order to reach the top, which is self-actualization. It is innate to want to advance as a person, but Maslow argues this cannot be done successfully if the supportive foundation found at the bottom of the pyramid is not tended to. These basic needs include air, food, shelter, warmth, etc (McLeod). For many, these needs are not met. How will they ever stay motivated and be successful? It's by working to have these needs met. Sometimes it requires the help of others to succeed in this regard. Unfortunately, when these needs are not met in childhood, the person must work that much harder to become a positive story. It can be done. Working to fulfill these needs is not a selfish act. It is what is necessary in order to reach self-actualization. At that level, people can truly be confident enough in themselves to then begin making a positive difference for others.

Successful Thoughts:

You are the product but the byproduct is your ability that everyone want to use.

Focus on self and in time others will want to follow, only when you are successful.

To see more encouraging and motivational thoughts go to page **69.**

The Real Enemy - *The Inner-Me*

Exercise:

I can see my future!! Write down where you see yourself in 5, 10, 15 and 20 years. In order to get there you have to see yourself in those places, careers, vacations and lifestyle.

In 5 years I will be…	
In 10 years I will be…	
In 15 years I will be …	
In 20 years I will be…	

Successful Thoughts:

Releasing from mental entrapment is the ability to tell yourself that no one is making you hold on to painful, people, experiences and thoughts.
Let it go and be free.

A leader can express themselves in times of adversity because they know that it is the best advice for the situation.

Be a master of your desire, know it like backward and forward.
Knowledge is power to use.

*To see more encouraging and motivational thoughts go to page **69**.*

Chapter 8

Releasing Mental Entrapment
Understanding who you are!!!

Chapter 8

Releasing Mental Entrapment
Understanding who you are!!!

Releasing Mental Entrapment is not simple but it is a relief from the obligation to others and accepting your own accountabilities. To release is to let go of something or someone and that is hard to do when you desire someone. It is easier to release when there is no desire for the thing or person. Why is it so hard to let go of things that may not be good for you? It may be because of your commitment level and because there is a desire to be needed and loved. If the wrong people fill that desire then the search for fulfillment continues and runs the risk of it being filled from anyone common. "The desire for love is so imperative that if it is not filled correctly with genuine love, then any substitute that appears and feels like love will be acceptable." This statement suggests the level of commitment through love. It is hard to let go of harmful people and things that are not good for us because we feel loved and desire from the substitute. Substitutes can and will allow you to acquire mixed emotions and misguided perspectives of reality and people. I want to tell you truth so you can be free from your entrapments. IT WAS YOUR FAULT.

It was your fault because you did not read this book as a child! LOL! You also did not listen to your parent and authority figure that did give their advice about life. You chose to do it your way based on your feelings and/or peers. Please take responsibility. I do understand that there are exceptions to the rule such as: parent abuse, parent and family rape, and child abuse both mentally and physically. Although these are serious offenses, we still have to find the way to release ourselves from the self-affliction and blaming, but when you use the experience as a tool to use in relationships to not do it again, then you have release from mental entrapment. Releasing from mental entrapment is a personal desire from the heart to gain a different way of thinking and lifestyle. Change. Change is how we as a human race evolve in every aspect of life.

The Real Enemy - *The Inner-Me*

> **Successful Thoughts:**
>
> Your passion is attached to your talent, your talent is attached to your skills, your skills is attached to your career, your career is attach advancement and advancement is attached to self-employment and self-employment is attached to a peace of mind and happiness,
>
> Life Motto: practice, hard work, talent, skills, commitment, dedication, new opportunities and change of life style. Then show someone else and hope they want it too.
>
> No one is born to without hope.
>
> Emotions requires investigation before a response. This save you from having to apologize for the mixed emotions.
>
> *To see more encouraging and motivational thoughts go to page* **69.**

Exercise: 👉

If you can change some things about yourself what would they be and why would you change them. Will they have a positive outcome in your life and what type of outcome would it be. How long will it take to make those changes?

What would you change?	What would be the positive outcome of the change?	How long will it take to make those changes?

The Real Enemy - *The Inner-Me*

The desire for change is like wanting a breath of air and without the oxygen you will die. Although this is not literal, it suggests that change is important and is a need for life to exist. **Change is the only constant thing that happens in all our lives. Here are some reasons for change to help with releasing yourself from mental entrapment:**

- Change is constantly happening.
- Change is logical understanding to improving self.
- Change is essential for the advancement of all people.
- Change your thought process and you can change your outcome.
- Change is improvement from one stage to a greater understanding about the same thing.
- Change is a desire to evolve.
- Change for the better is a change for the good of society.
- Positive change is for the good of self.
- Change is a wake-up call to develop a new ability to perform.
- Change your mind, change your perception, change your behavior, and the greatness in you will be life and love. Love yourself, others, and treat everyone as you want to be treated.

Releasing from a mental trap is to understand what that trap was made to do, then to identify the need for the trap, then understand how not to fall for the same trap twice. The purpose of this book is to do just that: identify an undesirable area in life that happens and realize sometimes it is because of ourselves and our feelings about it. This can cause a wrong decision. Many wrong decisions made in the past don't leave just because we grow up; most of the time it never leaves and we become challenged by it. It creates distrust with others. These false perceptions are due to personal, unpleasant, and negative experiences. The same principles work for an accurate or positive perception due to good experiences, and in comparison the same amount of energy and thought it takes to use the negative perception is the same energy it takes to be positive in perception. The mind is not meant to be wasted on hurt, pain, and self-affliction, but it is meant to be used as a creative tool to learn and use your mental and physical ability to sow, to work, to produce, and to reap the rewards of your input. The mind is powerful but if misused or not used it is wasted. The mind's power has the ability to influence self and others to do, think, or suggest with an expected result.

In addition, the mind has the ability to overcome situations, obstacles, and negative thoughts, but it has to be a desire from the heart. The mind is the determining factor of your intent and the results that you desire come from your heart. Our heart is determined by the words we speak, so by saying positive things others will know your intentions are good. By saying negative things people will know your intention are not good. Be careful with words you use. For out of the mouth, the tongue is like a two-edged sword and it can determine if you live or die. This biblical paraphrase implies

The Real Enemy - *The Inner-Me*

that the tongue or our words will express how we think and will either cause a positive or negative result. This is a fact that we are trapped due to our misunderstanding and limited knowledge about the current situation based on feeling and experiences. To relieve yourself, see the positive in the situation regardless of how negative it may seem. Why? To save your emotions from feeling negative, use your mind. The mind is the most powerful aspect of the human body. The power to influence is the ability to see the opportunity within the problem. The mind produces knowledge. Knowledge is the ability to think and process information in order to be excellent in performance or to gain more than you have. Knowledge is power and the more you gain the more you increase your ability to adapt and advance through life's experiences, which develop a strong communicator with charisma's power.

Charismatic power is the ability to use words and associations to employ a defining point. Charismatic people are very persuasive and can use words with insight and are creative to gain an advantage point. Power is everything and I want to suggest to use it with good intentions. A good use of this power is to always be open and honest, be flexible, become a mentor, speak and lead by example, and think before your speak.

Releasing mental entrapment is through the use of your mind. It is the power of the mind that will always allow you to overcome many things and challenges that will happen in life. The challenges are for us to encounter in order to learn from and overcome humbly and with the willingness to endure and learn, so when it occurs again we will be able to overcome it and help someone else. Relieve yourself from your past challenges but be thankful that you endured the experience because it will help in the future from being naïve, foolish, and easily manipulated about the same thing or something similar. KNOWLEDGE IS POWER and with this POWER YOU can be mentally free.

Power is the ability to have self-control, to influence a person or situation. Power only gives you the rights to be influential, but it does not mean you control another personal. The position use of power will reach more people and achieve goals. The misuse of power has repercussions. Knowing makes the difference. Knowledge increase your power. Knowledge is what you need to do and make better decision to improve yourself. It is your choice to use YOUR MIND to achieve good things and become more POWERFUL because of your INTENTION to do GOOD for YOUR LIFE.

YOU ARE NOW RELEASED FROM MENTAL ENTRAPMENT!

Chapter 9

Moments
My gift to the reader.

The Real Enemy - *The Inner-Me*

Chapter 9

Moments
My gift to the reader

In life we are given time to share special moments. The moments are meant for us to express our care and love that we feel for each other and that is when the moment starts.

Creating the moment requires for one or both people to feel compelled to be together because of a missed desired to see each other.

Communicating creates a moment: communication affirms the passion and desire for the moment to occur. Communication edifies a compassion that is built up and longs for a missed human touch.

The journey creates the moment and traveling throughout the journey creates the image of how one feels and since the last moment spent, which creates a stronger desire for touch to happen.

Travel allows time and space to combine which turns hope into reality.

The epic moment happens. This moment speeds up time and space because you are closer to seeing the person as you step into their presence; time allows the heart to rejoice and beat rapidly. An overwhelming feeling of relief moves within the heart and sends a message to the brain that communicates to the optical nerves. It signals your eyes to shed tears of joy, love, comfort, and a feeling of warmth because love is reached. United, it has filled its desire to reach the soul.

This moment is the moment I'm having for you. I LOVE YOU and hope you love yourself enough to change in order to improve and gain what has been yours since you were born. You were born to be POWERFUL and FREE.

SET YOURSELF FREE FROM MENTAL SLAVERY. YOU ARE FREE!

Bonus

Encouraging and Motivational Words
by Anthony Mckinley
Succesful Positive Thoughts

The Real Enemy - *The Inner-Me*

Bonus

Encouraging and Motivational Words
by Anthony McKinley
Successful Positive Thoughts

The following statements are my personal writing that I needed to help me on my journey and it helped me develop the core purpose of my writing.

Each statement suggests a state of mind and behavior to realize my POWER. This POWER is within all of us and it aids in everything from personal healing to changing the perception about self, life, and others. We all have the POWER to change and better ourselves. Discover your POWER within!

As you read you become more inspired to empower yourself to be successful in life. Your life is important.

Life Successful thoughts are to encourage you to strive with a plan to do well.

Life Successful Thoughts:

1. Living is for those whose desire is to make an impact.
2. Live life as a preparation for tomorrow.
3. Making it in life is up to you.
4. Mental entrapment is the lack of ability to accept and cope with life's realities.
5. Plan today for your life and for your children because they should benefit from it.
6. Plan, Prepare, Position, Produce, and Prosper are secrets to success.
7. You make the difference in your own life.
8. Your life is a selfish act when it comes to your lifestyle.
9. The condition of life doesn't mean it is the result of your destiny.
10. If it is to be it is up to me to make life better.
11. Life is fear; we all have opportunities to improve ourselves.
12. Life is a competitive race and only the strong will endure to the end and succeed.
13. No one should have to live their life in the shadow of hurt, lies, and secrets.
14. Life is full of mistakes, just admit it, apologize, and don't do it again.

The Real Enemy - *The Inner-Me*

15. Every lesson in life teaches and empowers all of us to do better and punishments are to inform all of us that it is wrong and to stop doing it before it is too late.
16. Life is not fair all the time. There are many disappointments you will encounter along the way but if you are fair in all your ways, then life will bless you the same.
17. No one is immune to the errors and trials in this life. If you fall down, get up and try again until you get it right.
18. Life is about continuous strength to survive with the will of determination to move forward positively through all adversities.
19. Only the strong will be victorious, and the race of life is not given to anyone.
20. It is an understanding that doing well can reap benefits that add to your character and credits your actions and the benefit of making decisions.
21. All things happened in the past to prepare for future actions to help someone else.
22. Speak life and love over yourself and it will happen as long as you practice it daily with an awareness to manifest it.
23. We are not alone in life; rely on someone who can help.
24. Being alive is not enough to understand the importance of becoming a contributor with intent.
25. Discovering your purpose in life is worth the journey you will experience and the accomplishments you will achieve.
26. What you give is what you will receive but how good and pleasant it is will be determined by your attitude and intention.
27. Each person's manifestation of things is the relevance of their practicality.
28. Life is about knowing the truth about things you are not familiar with, admitting your lack of knowing, and seeking the answer.
29. In life, the autonomy of the individual must not be denied. The personality will manipulate real aspects of personal perspective, which will automatically convert to familiarities that may be illusive dogma.
30. If you are going to fight for your life, then fight harder than the next man, because he is fighting too.
31. There are situations in life that will be used to bend and pressure your character to pull out your will of self-control and maturity.
32. You can't have commitment without being tested.
33. You can't desire to change without being tested on the very thing you want to change from. Pass the test.
34. If you fail your character test with change, it will surface again continuously until you pass the test. The test is a personal pass.

The Real Enemy - *The Inner-Me*

35. All tests are designed for everyone to pass and move to the next level.
36. Giving transforms you, the giver, within the self, family, and community.
37. Two types of giving: benevolent and vanity. When giving benevolently, it's from the heart with no expectations of a thank you. When giving in vanity, there is an expectation of receiving something in exchange or in return, but say it up front.
38. Life is let a track meet; there are other runners wanting the same goal: to be #1. The difference between each of you is not the talent but the development of the talent and work ethic.
39. No plan for your life is not a plan at all. You deserve better.
40. What happens to you between life and death will determine what your family and people think of you.
41. Live life with the intention to make and leave a mark or impression for the good of society.
42. Growth always involves the risk of failure or fulfillment. You have the potential.
43. As soon as you make the decision everything else falls in place.
44. There are going to be challenges in life but the focus should not be the problem, but what you are to learn from the situation.
45. We are a form of life that impacts the environment just like fruit and flowers.
46. A radical movement or disappointment sometimes has to occur to get us to move out of the comfort zone.
47. Everything in life is meant to have a positive outcome. It requires the ability of desire to think and speak life to all situations without excuses.
48. No one can make you do the right thing. It's a choice, and it's already in you. Activate it.
49. You better ask somebody if you don't know already!
50. Without change we all would be messed up.
51. A misunderstanding about life can cause resistance toward others and make you feel as if you don't fit in. Don't be afraid to learn a different way of seeing things.
52. There are four angles to a square. Develop your thought process before jumping to conclusions.
53. Don't be afraid of learning something you were wrong about.
54. There is a secret within learning something new.
55. We all are rewarded according to the measure of our talent, so develop it to get your worth.
56. Delight yourself in all moments of each day.
57. Your past has shaped your present perception and if something

The Real Enemy - *The Inner-Me*

         does not change, some things will hinder your future because of the wrong perception and understanding.

58. When you are fighting others, you may be fighting yourself. Evaluate your perception and logic.
59. The problem might be you and your perception. Check your perception with truth.
60. We are in need of others who tell the truth about your personality! Why? To develop your social independence as a productive citizen to become a leader.
61. We are jewels to each other, but you have to learn how to maintain it until it reaches its full potential.
62. We are always entertained, surrounding, and receiving signs to help us, and you have to be seeking to receive the sign.
63. In order to do anything, it is important to be effective in cultivating through network events/affairs and maintaining an effective relationship with everyone and without people there is no success.

Love successful thoughts are to encourage you during the challenging times.

Love Successful Thoughts:

1. Love is unconditional; stop putting conditions on things because those are limitations.
2. Life has turns and straight lines, but you're the driver.
3. Love is the most essential need for everyone.
4. Give from the heart and it will return to you.
5. Love is a need that we all desire and if it is not taught then we will accept any substitute that looks and feels like it. Hurt is not love.
6. Unconditional love means that you are not a condition to love.
7. Loving yourself first is the step to enlightenment!
8. Love is ME!
9. Love is an innate ability and it is intentional.
10. Love is the ability to take care of yourself in a positive manner and to treat others the same way: out of love.
11. Love is unconditional which means there are no circumstances that will stop you from loving yourself and others.
12. Some attributes of love include: Love does not cause hurt or pain to yourself or others. Love will allow you to tell the truth to others and find a way to be respectful.
There is one word that surpasses all others and that is love.
Love is selfish when it comes to personal achievements.

The Real Enemy - *The Inner-Me*

Love is constructive when others are giving advice to help you.
Love is benevolence, not vanity. Love is affectionate and not harsh.
Love is patience and kindness.
Love is letting go of others, habits, and things when they appear to be pleasant but in fact are harmful and self-destructive.
Love does not cost anything. Love is understood as charity.
Love is the only word that gives: it exudes peace and a greater understanding. Remember if it is not love then apologize and make the correction.

13. We are all created out of love! Love is the beauty that resides in every human being.
14. Love is the highest form of compassion, affection, and influence.
15. Love rules!
16. Unconditional love is not conditional love. It is inclusive verses exclusive.
17. The awakening of love is like setting goals; you have to achieve the success.
18. Love through it all and if it is to be, then it is up to us to make love present daily. Love is the ability to create it daily for self and others.
19. Love is an action that requires Love.
20. Loving yourself is a good, selfish action that every person needs to understand about life.
21. Love does not cause hurt and pain, people do.
22. Love is the ability to let go of someone or something in order to allow both them and yourself a change to have life.
23. Making love is mental, physical, intimate, in tune with life, and another person or your life goals enough to make an impactful difference to improve self, others, and processes.
24. Love is having a requirement: to give love to receive love.
25. Love is what we all are searching for but be selective.
26. Love yourself enough to be selfish about your well-being and success.

Work successful thoughts are to help propel you to reach the next level.

Work Successful Thoughts:

1. Causes and Effects: Action, Reaction, and Action.
2. Family is unity. We have to create the opportunity to plant seeds into our youth.
3. You have to plan your days or you are just living in the motion of whatever happens.

The Real Enemy - *The Inner-Me*

4. Please move out of your own way, let the past be the past and know that you can change your current situation if you change how your see it. Admit to your wrongdoing and decide to CHANGE and win your life back with a new perception. You are worth the work you invest into YOU.
5. Peace, Love and Will Power is a secret formula for success.
6. Work is part of life but at what cost do you not step up and accept a leadership role?
7. Leadership is an innate and developed ability but you have to invest in understanding the concepts, philosophies, and principals of being an effective leader.
8. Think strategically and it will raise your awareness and support to be able to master the task.
9. It is not just who you know but what you know too for the fit to match. Don't underestimate people in positions of power!
10. Don't get so caught up on work and money that you forget about self and family. Keep your values and prioritize.
11. It is a human need to be cared for and loved. If you don't do it for each other, someone else will. Give 100% to your own family first.
12. Don't kick a person while they are down but pull them up and encourage them to get striving with a positive attitude.
13. If you are not sure about something, then search for the answers and commit to finding the answer by giving your all because it is to make yourself satisfied and aware.
14. Work hard today, wake up and do it again until it happens.
15. No one can stop or hinder me, but me!
16. Work your plan today, do more the next day, and after until the plan is manifested into reality.
17. Five steps to a success process: follow, lead, train, own, and duplicate your business.
18. New things are never accepted until it is proven to work.
19. Practice proves it works.
20. New challenges are a sign of progress that you are ready. Walk in confidence and do it.
21. There is a difference between enhancing and eliminating a person's character.
22. CEO, Presidents, and Founders are always looking for YOU! Are you what they are looking for? That is the question.
23. CEO, Presidents, Founders, and Managers are looking for the next top, smart, flexible, teachable, sharp, and career-driven person to hire. Are you ready to be selected?
24. If you are not willing to endure pressure, prove your point of

justification with facts and stand up for your defense. Then you are ready to lead.
25. The ability to articulate your thoughts is critical to leadership and relationships.

Successful thoughts are to encourage you to fulfill the plan for you to accomplish to change your life.

Successful Thoughts:

1. Have a plan A only and work through the challenges to receive the rewards from the accolades called knowledge and wisdom. This helps with doing it yourself.
2. Success is determined by your action steps.
3. Success is time + plan = action; action + planned time = implementation; implementation + effective planning meeting = successful result.
4. STOP for self-study time for opportunities to progress.
5. Being selfish about goals, ambitions, and inspirations about your life is not something to be ambiguous about, but it should be something that is of importance and accomplishments for self.
6. Being able to make decisions about your life is essential and imperative to self and you should be careful about who you allow in your personal circle.
7. Money is only as good as what its value is worth and use is!
8. Prioritize yourself and plan your personal goals, career goals, and fill each one with a timeline.
9. The challenges we face today is the peace of mind for the future to help someone else.
10. There is a thin line between life and death both in the literally, metaphorically, and spiritual understanding of separation.
11. Never let your emotional anger be seen in public; it can cost you freedom.
12. Self-control is your ability to tame your temper and implement your coping skills.
13. Nothing is stopping a person from succeeding if they want to succeed.
14. Achievements are milestones that prepare you for the next level. Get ready for the next level.
15. It is never enough to wait on someone to do something for you when you can do it for yourself.
16. Don't be afraid to learn something new for personal growth.

The Real Enemy - *The Inner-Me*

17. Unleash the chains of doubt within yourself and replace it with courage and confidence because of what you know.
18. Doubting is an unacceptable habit that is not fit for any human being if they want to live with love and confidence.
19. Making the best of each day and night is the most effective way to love yourself and spouse.
20. Prepare for the doubt stuff to happen.
21. Be prepared to be tested in life and strive to pass each time, even if you failed the first time.
22. Discovering who you are is the greatest gift to yourself.
23. Life is nothing more than a competitive race for jobs, careers, retirement, and the winner will be the best performer who trained and prepared to be the best.
24. To be the best, you must know who you are, what your goals are in life, strive through practice, and always ask for help and training to reach your full potential and success.
25. To be good is not just saying it; it is the ability to prove it to others. Good is not self-proclaiming but only exists when others witness your achievements.
26. An opportunist seeks the chance to do and strives with their mind to create their life with greater possibilities.
27. Practice, practice, and more practice will help create winners.
28. Your goals motivate your desires and drive.
29. One way to identify your good nature is through meditation. Take that time for yourself.
30. You can't receive anything if you are not giving to yourself.
31. Seeking it until it happens means you have to have a daily desire to get what you're seeking. Never stop.
32. There is a cost for life and love. Nothing is free.
33. You have permission to go behind challenges or anything, but you have to think and seek the understanding on a higher level behind your current understanding.
34. We are born to solve problems, not cause problems. Solve the problem.
35. We are born to improve and advance humanity, not cry and worry about what not to do.
36. There are resolutions to ambiguous condition.
37. No ideas, no impartation, conceptualization, no implementation equals no gratification, no advancement, and no economic or personal gain. You have to have a drive to learn and lead.
38. To become an entrepreneur or become the best version of yourself: you must have the drive to learn, implement, lead, instruct, and

The Real Enemy - *The Inner-Me*

      replicate the concept and become the entrepreneur and owner of your invested gift.

39. We are all gifted but we must invest in developing our talents to be effective in using the gifts.
40. Just because you are born does not mean that you are better than the next person. We all have to prove ourselves worthy.
41. Anything you desire for yourself, you must be willing to put in the time, work, late nights, and early mornings or lost sleep just so you can reach the goal and begin to live in your destiny.
42. Life is like the desire for air, without a desire you are dead.
43. Everyone is given the same opportunities in life but you have to listen and pay attention to the signs and encouragement that surround you in a positive environment.
44. You have the power to make the opportunity available but you have to strive and endure all of life's adversities and stay focused on your goal.
45. It is not meant for everyone to believe in but it is meant for you to believe in yourself.
46. If you don't see pain as a character builder and see the challenges as opportunities, you will always misread and misunderstand the action of the terms overcame, your perseverance, and your achievements.
47. True conquest spreads over a lifetime.
48. There is a thin line between success and failure; you have to merge the gap.
49. When you start something, know there will be distractions designed to deter you from your focus goal, but cross the finish line for your completed goal.
50. Distractions are designed to strengthen your commitment level in order for you to achieve.
51. We are taught to follow rules and step up to leadership, so why do we put ourselves down? Step up, and mark your territory.
52. Failure has never been an option but it is a choice.
53. Choose to love through it all with a positive mind state.
54. Making it in life is easy but if you have bad experiences, it is just more challenging. Reeducate yourself and surround yourself around positively thinking people.
55. Second place is not winning. That is ok, but it will never be first place until you value being the best and strive to be #1.
56. There is nothing in life that supports the idea that second place is the driven goal. First place is a reflection of your hard work and determination.
57. It is hard being on top all the time, but it is worse being second and never knowing how it feels to be the leader.

The Real Enemy - *The Inner-Me*

58. Success is the desire to live.
59. Winners never give up and those who want to be a winner work harder than the last winner.
60. Winners never stop at second and always work to be first in achieving their personal goals.
61. Believe in yourself and abilities enough to invest, develop, and use it to get money.
62. Some selfishness is what every person needs to achieve in life.
63. Success is determined by your personal goals and once you achieve, others will strive to succeed too.
64. Running your first race is not about just saying you did it; it is about finishing the race and preparing to be better the next time.
65. You are as great as you want to be by your invested talent and implementation.
66. Roman numeral 1 is self-explanatory and everything else is not desirable.
67. Make time for yourself to plan out your life to reach the next level because it affects the lives of others too.
68. What are you willing to sacrifice to gain what is good for your life?
69. There is always room at the top. It's called the winners' circle.
70. Money is an expensive habit if it is wasted, but money can be a game changer if you invest in profitable stock.
71. The price of gain is vision, commitment, belief and the will power to believe in yourself and abilities. Are you prepared for the enormous moment to gain?
72. To be aimed at is to say that you are watched and it can be looked at as an opportunity to shine versus being called out. Knowledge is power in these situations.
73. Being prepped, prepared, and patient with a plan is the opportunist's way.
74. Write your manifesto because you are a brainchild genius and the future depends on it.
75. One of most interesting and enormously important people is you. Act like it.
76. Act like your goals until they become who you are in reality.
77. Merit treatment is not established by saints or devils but by the intention of the act.
78. Successful clarity illuminated and interpreted by others is why people invest in people and product.
79. The world is occupied by revolutionary people. Be one too.
80. Your plan will never bear too much fruit during your lifetime.

The Real Enemy - *The Inner-Me*

81. The final imprint of life will determine what we did while we were young and dogmatic.
82. Predict your life and income level and it will be inevitably. Rise to the occasion.
83. See the future. I had to win.
84. A leader is always striving to walk ahead of time.
85. Leadership gives us each life. It's a dominating trend, which becomes an essential, not a casual or part of our character.
86. Riches come with maturing, discipline, and commitment to not spend on want but only for necessities.
87. Prerequisites are needed for the next advancement.
88. Don't take short cuts in your career because you can leave out one vital point and it's over.
89. Your passion is attached to your talent, your talent is attached to your skills, your skills are attached to your career, your career is attached to advancement, and advancement is attached to self-employment. Self-employment is attached to a peace of mind and happiness.
90. Life Motto: practice, hard work, talent, skills, commitment, dedication, and new opportunities will result in a change of life style. Show someone else and hope they want it too.
91. No one is born without hope.
92. Emotions require investigation before a response. This saves you from having to apologize for the mixed emotions.
93. Everyone is given that chance to experience life, so why not live in pleasure?
94. How well you prepare for a day will determine how you handle unforeseen situations.
95. Leading is not as easy as you think. In your hands as a leader people expect you to make the best decision and the responsibilities are enormous, but you can do it as long as you trust in the truth and are willing to adjust.
96. Anyone can talk success but it means nothing if you can't back it up with a paycheck and lifestyle.

The Real Enemy - *The Inner-Me*

Inspirational successful thoughts should inspire you to think and have positive thoughts about life.

Inspirational Successful Thoughts:

1. Plan your days, complete your task, and do it again the next day.
2. Joy is from within to share with others.
3. If heaven is a place that you desire to be, then create it on Earth for others to see.
4. YET-predict things to come because of your action in motion.
5. Never give in, never give up, and always give your best.
6. Night is a perfect time for meditation and self-reflection.
7. Everyday alive is a new opportunity to reach your personal goals.
8. Wake up with an intention for your day.
9. Today is a new day to do something new.
10. Make it happen, TODAY!
11. Make it work, TODAY!
12. The Journey of Faith: Implementation of your Will.
13. Change your perception, change your behavior, and change your understanding about life. Nothing is impossible!
14. Start at the beginning and you will find the ending the same.
15. Pray over yourself and be encouraging about your future.
16. Speak positive words to yourself and to others and it will return to you.
17. The conditions of the world are only conditions, but they don't have to determine your outcome. These conditions change because of love.
18. Regardless of your current situation, we were all born into this world for a purpose and to love and enjoy life with a peace of mind and a sense of self-accomplishment.
19. It is OK to admit that you don't know yourself, but don't act like you do in public and make a questionable fool of yourself. Learn so you can speak with confidence.
20. Knowing makes the difference in behavior, understanding, and the will to do for self and others, and if you don't know then find out first and then act or respond.
21. Know yourself and prove to yourself that you can do anything when you put your mind to it, and everyone else will see it too.
22. If you don't have anything to prove, then you are not living within the circle of life.
23. We are all born to be great but for greatness one must be willing and able to prove themselves by becoming good, better, and great.
24. During painful times, do not give up but endure through it.

The Real Enemy - *The Inner-Me*

25. Having is the same as giving. Sowing is reaping.
26. Someone else's inappropriate behavior or action is designed to mature you, and the same in reverse: your mature behavior and action is designed to mature them. Lead by example.
27. I am what I demonstrate within self, to my family, at work, and in public. Become ONE with self.
28. Endurance is the same as deliverance.
29. Working to self-improve is the true meaning of good.
30. We are ONE as a race of people.
31. Find your passion for life and STOP causing spiritual suicide.
32. The things that you will do for free is attached to your passion.
33. It is important to understand the things that you struggle with so one day you can help someone else with the same things. (Following and then you lead.)
34. If you are not able to stand in the times of challenges then no one will need you. We all want someone who we can depend on during the good and challenges, not a coward.
35. YOU are important to life as a concept.
36. A philosopher is established in every human being, but it has to be activated.
37. I can do all things because I was born to live, give, and receive forgiveness and love only to show and demonstrate my desire and skills too.
38. Total affirmation cancels out by the overwhelming power of the act of fundamental contradictions: the TRUTH.
39. The truth is a positive mind state that provokes an enlighten moment to cause a conscious awareness of Self to evolve.
40. Integrity of assent creates intimacy behind measure.
41. In times where your character and reputation are in crisis, the act of commitment pulls and takes a moment to yield to the consent in silence.
42. I receive with thanksgiving and appreciation. Thank you!
43. Don't have friends that are your cheerleaders and "yes" men.
44. If you're the smartest in your friend circle: how do you expect to learn and grow personally?
45. Needs are essential and sometimes given, but to have an abundance requires more of yourself as it pertains to developing your talent, putting plans together to implement, and being trusted.
46. Trust is given to everyone, freely, but when you break it, you have to make the correction to build the trust up again.
47. Pretending is dangerous, because your true identify is discovered. Then you have disappointed people who believed and trusted in you.

The Real Enemy - *The Inner-Me*

48. Words are effective but how you use them will determine the effectiveness of the words.
49. Strive to become impeccable within your character.
50. Every day you live you have an opportunity to do things better or invest in yourself.
51. I am a positive person and I will live this day to say something nice.
52. My positive vibe will impact the people that come into contact with me daily.
53. It takes one day to receive or make a first impression even if it is with a familiar place or people.
54. There will always be more prophets that impact people to do great things to help society.
55. Once we're accepted by ourselves, we become meaningful.
56. Knowing yourself is the total meaning of discovery and love.
57. You are the source of an expression so speak it well and say it loudly, "I am ME."
58. Own up to your mistake so people can see the mistake but also see that you are an honest person, and one who learns from the lesson.
59. You are born gifted and at work and at home you are needed to do well, so have fun but be safe.
60. If you don't want to be needed then you are selfish and missing the purpose of companionship with others.
61. None of us are an island so let's work together when it is required.
62. God is not biased; there is a reason for everything.
63. We forgive because we want to be forgiven.
64. If I want to treated a certain way, I must make sure that I am treating everyone the way I want to be treated.
65. Life is easy if you think about how you want to give and do it with love with no expectations from people for your actions.
66. I have the power to make a difference today!
67. Releasing from mental entrapment is the ability to tell yourself that no one is making you hold onto painful people, experiences, and thoughts. Let it go and be free.
68. A leader can express themselves in times of adversity because they know it is the best advice for the situation.
69. Be a master of your desire. Know it backward and forward. Knowledge is power to use.
70. Never be a yes man if it is not true. Most people know that something is not the best thing for the situation, but they are hoping that someone can be innovative and creative to suggest something better. Be the one and make sure that it is factual.
71. Be the call person at your company because you have the skill and the vision.

The Real Enemy - *The Inner-Me*

72. Be an asset and not liability in anything that you do. Be dependable!
73. Have trust, faith, talent, developed skills, vision, and a voice to do everything you desire.
74. Don't live in the past of negative behavior patterns; it will only lead to a future filled with negativity.
75. Romance is in everything, but it does not mean sex, but sexuality.
76. If you are an independent thinker then stop relying on others who mislead you negatively.
77. You are born to be innovative, creative, and an inventor of things not seen yet. YET!
78. Making a statement is not being silent in the time of a storm.
79. Silence in most cases is required when you don't know. So listen and learn.
80. If you want to understand life, then do things to keep living to find out.
81. Find a reason to live and always find ways to do the same thing better.
82. Passing all tests is required if you want to improve yourself and life.
83. Life is a seeking addiction for happiness and love if you desire it.
84. Seeking is not timed and it requires never giving up until it is duplicated. Full cycle.
85. The power is your hands if you understand YOUR abilities and what to do with them.
86. Cause and effect is not an accident, so do things intentionally good and better.
87. If you are going to follow then you can follow and if you are going to lead then lead but make a choice with confidence in your abilities and based on your strengths.
88. Only you can make the difference in yourself; others just suggest things in your favor.
89. Social norms are important to understand as you develop and grow.
90. Trust is given based on your ability to trust.

The Real Enemy - *The Inner-Me*

Powerful successful thoughts are to provoke you to change your internal thoughts about life situation and encourage a new positive perception.

Powerful Successful Thoughts:

1. Mental entrapment is the lack of ability to accept and cope with life's realities.
2. Saying NO is the power of confidence.
3. Saying YES is sometimes to fit in, which is fake.
4. Never let anyone speak ill of your good character or works but if it is true then change it.
5. Giving is benevolent and vanity is with an expectation.
6. If you are worried about something, that means that you are aware and you have the ability to change it.
7. The Enemy is my Inner-me.
8. The Real Enemy is my inner self.
9. Remember to come back to the middle. There are three levels in the game of life: the beginning, the middle and the end. As difficult times come, always go back to the middle.
10. The power of the mind is as small or as large as we know and conceptualize.
11. It is not our responsibility to change someone else. It is hard enough just changing ourselves.
12. Mental Entrapment: If you accept and allow negative statements, thoughts, and stereotypes to consume your thoughts and behaviors then you cannot break the chains of oppression and self-destruction until you change your perception of life
13. Let no one speak ill about your good character.
14. Renew and reeducate yourself from mental slavery. No one can free you but YOU.
15. Mental entrapment is the lack of ability to let pain, hurt, and the lack of love go.
16. Striving with a dogmatic desire is sometime required to MOVE NOW.
17. Sometimes we do what we think is best today and apologize later if correction is needed. Make the decision.
18. Push through challenges and deal with things immediately to resolve them.
19. If your intention is not love, then it is hate and that must change. Not one is born to hate.
20. Don't be stuck in the middle of your life; get up and make a decision.

The Real Enemy - *The Inner-Me*

21. Words hurt, so think before you speak and apologize if you're in the wrong because of your perception, emotion, or lack of understanding.
22. People who take time out for you and encourage you to do well love and care about you as a human being and person.
23. A bad man is a bad man if he thinks he is! A good man is a good man if he thinks he is! It takes the same amount of energy for both and you have the power of choice.
24. Please believe that we are all inherently good and that doing well is an innate ability that all human beings possess.
25. True honor comes when someone has done something good with respect, pride, and discipline.
26. Make this a personal rule: only depend on your own abilities and listen to others' positive constructive advice. Positive constructive advice is good, if it is meant to help you do something better or achieve something you have never achieved positively.
27. Personal selfishness has to do things for self-satisfaction, and everyone must be willing to do things for self because when everything and everyone is gone you must be happy with yourself and the things done within each day.
28. We are imperfect people and have made many mistakes and without the mistakes we would not know what to look for the next time it happens. It has been said it is better to listen to others' advice and guidance rather than making mistakes.
29. Mental entrapment is a self-destructive act.
30. You only can change yourself and others have to change for themselves too. It is not our responsibility to change someone else. It is hard enough just changing ourselves.
31. We as people must begin to understand that we can't help others until we help ourselves first.
32. Problem solving requires the TRUTH about the situation. The truth will set and make you free mentally.
33. If you make mistakes and you are punished for it, then you are supposed to learn from the experience as a lifelong lesson.
Don't do it again!
34. It is imperative that all children and adults understand parental laws and the law to survive in society.
35. Do the good things today and when you awake the next day it will return to you. You're the planter.
36. Planting seeds is what we are and what we plant will return, so be careful of the seeds you plant into others' lives.

The Real Enemy - *The Inner-Me*

37. Why do bad things happen to us? To prepare us for the next time it happens but what matters is how we handle it and not run from it. Stand and implement your good.
38. All good intentions are not taken as well if the other person is not ready to receive it, but don't give up on them, just learn to wait on them to ask for help.
39. Waiting on someone to ask for help is better than volunteering it, because they may not want your help and it becomes offensive. A good intention may result in a bad outcome.
40. STOP creating co-dependent people and blaming them when they don't become independent.
41. Stop, look, and listen before you respond with a negative word. Ask for clarity.
42. When you hear negative things, ask them to repeat it and ask what their intention was. This saves you from an emotional spin off.
43. Stop with giving into negative thoughts and do something positive.
44. If someone criticizes you, you have to choose to do something with it, but don't disregard the information because it could help you.
45. You are the incarnation and manifestation of God's desire. Believe it and live it daily.
46. The challenges we face today is the peace of mind we will have for self and to use in the future to help others.
47. Ruling self is the first rule of achievement for self.
48. In all situations, challenges blame self. Look at self to determine as an individual what you could have done differently first and second. Talk to each other about the experience to determine how to fix the situation to establish a common understanding and because love and understanding is the result we want.
49. Agree with your challenges quickly! Why? To resolve it and move on to next level of doing things.
50. The craziness that each person faces is to help them mature and do it better the next time.
51. If it is good then it is good for all.
52. Secrets are great to reveal when you are being vulnerable with others who are special to you.
53. Being transparent to the right people can change your path for the better.
54. Transparency creates open transparency, which helps with transforming you into who you want to be because you endure and achieved the transformation to better your life.
55. I want to live so bad that I will do things to stay positive, seek opportunities for self-development, and advance within leadership and receive all my earned rewards.

The Real Enemy - *The Inner-Me*

56. Money is not evil but what you do with the money is evil. The desire for money is not evil; the desire to do evil things is evil.
57. In all things have positive intentions, and you will have a positive outcome.
58. There is a Superior, Creator, God, Almighty and unique being greater than the human race, although the only proof is in faith and personal belief. When speaking truth to knowledge, we don't come from ourselves. Go backward in time and you SEE the TRUTH.
59. I give because I do want something in return and the best is love, kind words, and gifts.
60. Seeking is a never-ending process.
61. If you put me in a jungle to survive, I would, because I am designed to conquer all things and animals.
62. Nothing will ever happen just because you think of it; you have to put in the work and believe in yourself.
63. Unresolved issues are like a distrusted bee. It will come back to sting.
64. Deal with all situations quickly so you can move forward.
65. You are designed to learn, grow, and do well. STOP doubting yourself.
66. Learning is a lifelong process to achieve. The more you know the more you can adjust.
67. Be as an eagle that prepares to meet the wind intently to strengthen its wings and to become stronger.
68. Release from the chains of mental bondage. How? Change how you see the chains and know that it is not the chains that have you in bondage but it is you holding yourself in bondage. It's about your perception.
69. All men are created equal but others are more determined to have more than others to become the exceptional man.
70. The epic moment is when you and time meet for the first time. You are in the moment, and feel the air and the wind under your feet releasing from the old way of thinking. Then the break and transformation happen and you become something new because you believed, spoke it into existence, and lived it.
71. Speak all things that are concerning you and your desire well.
72. Knowing with confidence will determine how you feel.
73. Knowing and speaking with confidence to others based on fact will win others over.
74. You have everything to lose and the world to win, if you have the right intention.
75. There is a thin line between progress and poverty. The decision you make today will determine the truth of your action.
76. The truth is freedom and others will always know it. The truth doesn't lie.

The Real Enemy - *The Inner-Me*

77. Focus on self and in time others will want to follow, only when you are successful.
78. Don't read your own press. Set high standards and let others appreciate your doings and just say thank you.
79. Living and existing with people requires the ability to share.
80. No one is perfect but we do have some better ways that appear to look perfect.
81. Don't be pretentious. It is misleading and hurtful when others learn the truth about you.
82. A self-driven person is most likely to make it in life with the will to learn from others.
83. Motivation is the encouragement we all need to become innovative about our life and purpose.
84. You are the product but the byproduct is your ability that everyone wants to use.
85. Using others is what we all do. Please see things as it is and what you feel.
86. There is a difference between appeasement and pleasing but they both require the same action: passion and giving from the heart because you want to.
87. There is a right approach to everything you do and say.
88. There is always irrevocable truth but you have to seek and find it for yourself.
89. There are revocable truths but you need to know what is truth.
90. A rich man says to himself, "I need to compound my wealth."
91. In times of disagreement, ask yourself, "What could I have done differently?"
92. Learn to give the gift of financial security to your loved ones.
93. Compare and save yourself from negative thoughts and behavior.
94. Ask for help from trustworthy adults and elders.
95. A fool doesn't ever want to hear the truth, no matter who the source is.
96. The highest cost of dying is not paying for your own funeral.
97. Replacement is an irrevocable truth that will happen in one life span.
98. What should you expect from life? What you give to life. Make good decision.
99. We are all common but the difference is the next word. A common _____.
100. Don't be a boring person; have character and be adaptive.
101. Multinational is a worldwide vision when you talk about making impact.
102. The ability to transplant, reproduce, and process in areas of the world is a succeeding wish and it affects the economic world, but find a

The Real Enemy - *The Inner-Me*

way to stop money from exchanging its power and resulting in a depression.

103. What seems beyond doubt is that we must move things from the limited boundaries and provoke a new understanding with direction and improvements.
104. Nothing stops progress, not even man.
105. Vitalization, modern, and innovative ideas are what develops new competitiveness of the systems that suggest change.
106. Being perplexed is ambiguous. Make the best decision and live with it.
107. Learning is making mistakes and correcting them, but not learning is a mistake.
108. To admit that you have the presence, power, and obedience is activating your internal will and destiny.
109. So close but so far away, because it is not NOW.
110. Others never determine self-worth until you have to prove it. Be willing to provide what you believe.
111. Believing in your ability requires proving it over and over again. We all are required.
112. Proving your ability will determine if you are telling the truth to others.
113. How good you are is determined by performance against others doing the same thing.
114. Life is filled with uncertain things, and all things are designed for you to learn from both good and bad, but never for you to give up on yourself.
115. No one can live without the help from others, so STOP saying you don't need anyone or that you did it on your own. That is a lie. Open your eyes!
116. Speaking the truth requires thinking before you speak because you want others to do the same for you.
117. I am the life that I live and if I don't have what I want it is because I did not invest in myself to earn it for my existence.
118. I am not invisible. I am picture perfect.
119. I am what I think I am and I will prove it through my ability to demonstrate.
120. I am the reflection of life, love, and positive energy to share without opening my mouth.
121. I am a hybrid born to succeed.
122. All things matter if it requires influence.
123. Don't allow yourself to become a staving man. Learn how to fish for a lifetime.
124. There are repercussions to everything, so think before you speak.

The Real Enemy - *The Inner-Me*

125. Correct your erroneous situations.
126. Pride kills, but corrections create understanding.
127. Beware of followers that are pretending to be leaders. Use wisdom by questions.
128. Question all things, so you will know the truth with confidence.
129. If you don't know, then find out, so you can fit in.
130. Learning is a jewel with the right intention.
131. Waiting is stopping, so work while you wait. Please don't procrastinate.
132. Creativity is being out of the box.
133. Most great ideas were not done yet. YET!
134. A negative imagination, feelings, and perceptions are a distraction from truth. Know the truth by understanding the root of the fear and ask for or investigate the history of that negative pain.
135. We are healed once we realize it and believe it.
136. Restriction is a limitation of your knowledge bank, skill set, and the lack of ability to trust your own abilities.
137. Your mental perception and physical conditions will determine your health and drive to have and do. Love yourself to do for self.
138. Become who you want to be. It starts with you and your development.
139. A leader is one who can solve problems with integrity, handle controversy, and speak the truth based on facts.
140. Stop limiting yourself with the restriction found in the words, "I can't."
141. Limitation is an indication that you don't want anything else. Where is your hope?
142. Hope is the possibility of things to become evident in the future. Plan today.
143. Making things easy is a disservice to others learning to do. Hard work always pays off.
144. Stop with holding others to standards and hold yourself to standards to do well for yourself.
145. Do yourself the favor and achieve your goals. Support others that are trying too.
146. Wherever there is a problem, you have to power to solve it.
147. Relying on your emotion and logic, you stand a better chance to solve situations.
148. If you are treated unfairly, to change from it, you must make sure you're not doing the same thing to someone else.
149. It is your responsibility to strive to improve yourself.
150. Get to the next level.

The Real Enemy - *The Inner-Me*

151. It is not about my past but about my future.
152. Focus on where you are going and don't look back.
153. Looking back is backward and we are forward-thinking people.
154. It is our responsibility to move forward and reach the next level.
155. Desire to care about yourself enough to speak the truth all the time.
156. Giving up when you are ahead is not the same as giving up.
157. The best you give to others, will someday be the best returned to you.
158. Seek what you are asking for; it won't just come without you seeking to find it.
159. Rejections are redirections.
160. No one is immune to the uncertainties, hardship, and rewards life presents. It is no accident.
161. There are no accidents in life but there are new perceptions to gain as preparation for the next level of doing things.

Dream Successful Thoughts are to encourage you to strive and manifest your vision, and plans to reach your destiny and help yourself.

Dream Successful Thoughts:

1. Don't stop dreaming and visualizing until it becomes your reality.
2. Progress is moving forward with a goal and plan.
3. I am on my way. I may not know my final destination; however, I have had a preview and now I know I'm bound for greatness because I AM SOMEBODY.
4. The illusive illusion is realizing what real is, where reality is, and who it is about.
5. Search within yourself and discover your desires, dream, and make them your reality.
6. God, Self, Family and Friends. If married-God, Self and Spouse, Family, and Friends.
7. Dreams are nothing without learning and implementation for it to become the reality.
8. I am who I visualize, speak into existence and believe I am.
9. Great relationships require the following personal concepts: establishing rapport, developing strong communication, and maintaining the relationship over a period of time because of the value to grow and improve through life lessons.
10. We don't evolve because we maintain, we evolve because of the dreams

The Real Enemy - *The Inner-Me*

and visions that are not present yet. Your new ideas are relevant to the future advancement of human beings.

11. No man comes from himself and he is unable to create anything from nothing.
12. We are barriers of other things or people's ideas to expand upon.
13. Nothing is new but all things can be improved upon.
14. There is never a perfect time to make an impact. The perfect timing is always RIGHT NOW, TODAY!
15. Your hope and aspiration is your drive to be unique and become greater than your circumstance of tomorrow.
16. Dreams and visions are given for you to work toward; you create the opportunity because you put in the work to become the reality to reach your destiny. Seek and find.
17. Preview your life, review your goals, and live the vision.
18. A visionary writes, discusses, researches, reviews, and implements the vision for proof that it is real.
19. Don't just dream; create through innovation and creativity to bring the dream into reality.
20. The imagination is a powerful tool so use it to improve yourself or a situation.
21. You are what you think you are mentally, physically, and spiritually.

References

Deci, E. L., & Ryan, R. M. (2002). Overview of self-determination theory: An organismic dialectical perspective. In E. L. Deci & R. M. Ryan (Eds.), *Handbook of self-determination research* (pp. 3-33). Rochester, NY: University of Rochester Press.

McLeod, Saul. "Maslow's Hierarchy of Needs." Simply Psychology. N.p., 2007. Web. 02 Oct. 2014.

Rimm-Kaufam, Sara, PhD, UVA. "Improving Students' Relationships with Teachers to Provide Essential Supports for Learning." *Http://www.apa.org*. N.p., n.d. Web. 01 Oct. 2014.

Vesia, John. "The Real Enemy: Fighting the False Self." Martial Views. N.p., 3 Oct. 2005. Web. 12 Oct. 2014.

The Real Enemy - *The Inner-Me*

Personal and Inspirational Notes:

_____
_____
_____
_____
_____
_____
_____
_____
_____
_____
_____
_____
_____
_____
_____
_____
_____
_____
_____
_____
_____
_____
_____

The Real Enemy - *The Inner-Me*

Personal and Inspirational Notes:

_____
_____
_____
_____
_____
_____
_____
_____
_____
_____
_____
_____
_____
_____
_____
_____
_____
_____
_____
_____
_____
_____
_____
_____
_____
_____

Personal and Inspirational Notes:

www.ingramcontent.com/pod-product-compliance
Lightning Source LLC
Chambersburg PA
CBHW042024150426
43198CB00002B/59